PERSUASION GPS

Get to Where You Want to Go *Faster*

Lynne Franklin

THIN LEAF PRESS | LOS ANGELES

Cataloging-in-Publication Data
Names: Franklin, Lynne, Author
Title: *PersuasionGPS™: Get to Where You Want to Go Faster*

ISBN 978-1-953183-78-1 (paperback)
ISBN 978-1-953183-77-4 (eBook)

Professional Development, Communication, Self-Help, Success,

Thin Leaf Press
Los Angeles

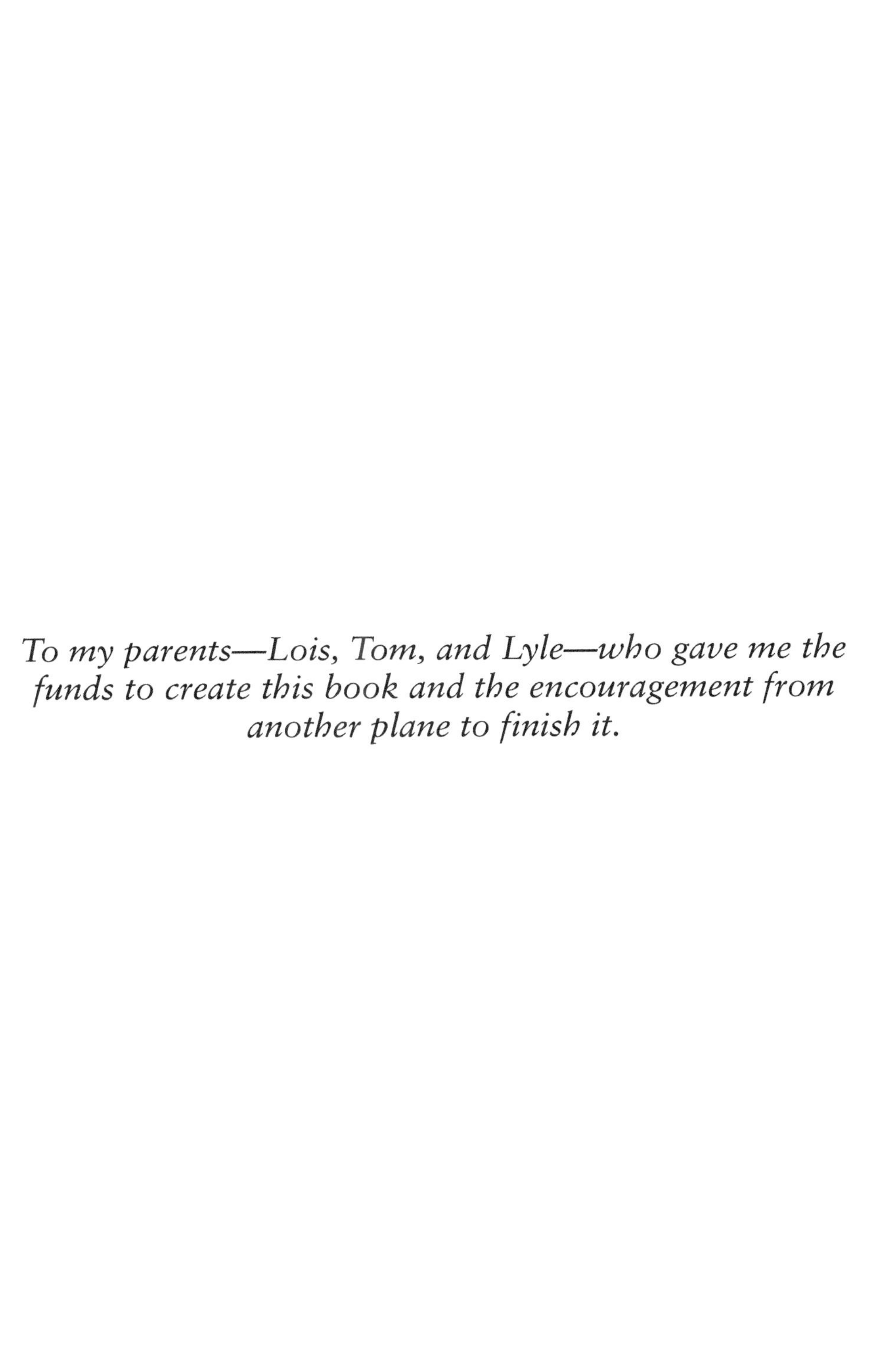

To my parents—Lois, Tom, and Lyle—who gave me the funds to create this book and the encouragement from another plane to finish it.

CONTENTS

INTRODUCTION

Persuasion isn't about getting everyone to say "yes" to you. It's about helping people make good decisions.

People often ask about the most important moment *I* needed to be persuasive.

For years, my answer was, "When a fourteen-year-old named Fred threatened to kill me with a machete." (More on this in the strategic stories section.) Chances are good that's never happened to you, but we all have a moment when we need to be persuasive.

For me, the machete situation was eclipsed by another, which is more common. Now I say, "When I had to tell my husband we needed to divorce."

CAUTION: GRAPHIC CONTENT AHEAD

Divorce? *That* was a turn you probably weren't expecting! "Isn't this a book about persuasion tools for your professional life?" you might be asking. If you've never been divorced, or don't plan to be, you might be thinking reading this isn't worth your time.

While I can't answer that for you, there are two things I *do* know.

First: everything you'll read here is about change. It requires changing your thoughts and actions by stopping rote behaviors and trying new approaches. If you're up to the challenge, this can be uncomfortable and often messy (kind of like a divorce). I'll do my best to make the roadmap clear and simple.

Second: you have no reason to believe any of this will work—unless I show you how it has for me. (Relax: the rest of the book illustrates how PersuasionGPS™ has helped others in business situations.). I'll start with the toughest talks I've had, which happen to be personal. If you value authenticity and vulnerability, you'll find it here. Sometimes you'll like me. Sometimes you'll think I'm bitchy. Sometimes you'll feel sorry for my ex-husband. But you'll know you're getting as close to the truth as I can share it.

Here's the gift to you for reading the next section: perspective. No matter how difficult the situation you apply this to at work, at least it's not as fraught as a divorce. And you'll also know this stuff works just as well in your personal life.

A TALE OF TWO TOUGH TALKS

After eight months of cortisone shots, pain pills, physical therapy, electrical stimulation—and now facing neck surgery—I was exhausted. Trying to quiet my brain one night to get to sleep, it hit me. "Maybe I'm just done with being *married.*"

When I woke the next morning, there was less pain. (The mind-body connection is great when you pay attention to it!)

Now what?

I grabbed a pen and paper and wrote three true things:

1. *Larry is a good man who has done things that show he can never be the right partner for me.*
2. *I don't need to punish him. I just need not to be married to him.*
3. *I want to come out the other side of this with a good relationship with Larry—without bankrupting myself to do it.*

How can I make this happen?

Tough Talk #1: Knowing the news would feel like a complete surprise to Larry, I thought about how to break it to him. We were in couples counseling. It seemed a good idea to tell him during a session, so he could have the support of our therapist. I spoke with her in advance and asked if she would be ready at our next session to help him work through the initial shock. She agreed.

Then it hit me. What would I say to him?

In fits of annoyance, I'd come up with long lists of things Larry had done to wrong me. Part of me would have loved the satisfaction of unleashing these on him, followed by "and *that's* why I can't be married to you!" Of course, that would violate all of the three of the true things I'd just written. There had to be another way.

When the evening for our session came, I swallowed hard, looked him in the eyes and jumped in—beginning with the story of how my back pain disappeared. I finished with, "If you can't be the partner *I* need, then I can't possibly be the one *you* need, either. I love you. I'll always love you. But I just can't be married to you."

Larry had been through an ugly divorce before. He would have said, done, or agreed to anything to prevent that from happening again. It was painful to watch him try to convince me I was wrong. That he would change, and everything would be OK. Part of me really wished that could be true.

So I replied with a list of the things I loved about him. His great sense of fun. His talent for graphic design. How easy he was to like and be with. His kindness to and enjoyment of the time we spent with my family.

Then I asked, "What do you love about me?"

Larry couldn't name a single thing. That's when I knew we were done as a couple.

What I hadn't planned for was the long, silent, and uncomfortable ride home afterward. Then there was the 10 months that followed, while we lived in our house until it was sold. The ugly outbursts, when he wanted to hurt me for all the pain he felt I was causing him. His occasional pretending that, once the house was sold, we would move into another and stay together. The refusal to have the two of us tell his daughter what was going on.

No matter how many times I wanted to retaliate, I kept those three true things in mind. Then I'd find another way to blow off the negative energy: from long conversations with friends I trusted, to the "brown thought cloud."

Brown Thought Cloud: Lots of people tell me this idea is one of their favorites, and they often use it.

Imagine this. Someone has said or done something in front of you that's really stupid, frustrating, or maddening. You'd love to call them out and tell them off. But if you do, it will make matters worse—and maybe damage a relationship. (Who wants to collaborate with you after you've eviscerated them?)

Picture yourself in a cartoon strip.

You have one of those thought bubbles with words above your head—the kind that no one else can see.

In my head, I color these brown, because they're filled with all the snarky, sarcastic comments you'd love to spew in the moment—but would get you in trouble if you did. Instead, say them to yourself, and silently laugh at how clever and amusing you are!

This releases the tension that's building up in you. (It has to go *somewhere*.)

What the rest of the world sees is that you pause. This gives the impression that you're patiently considering something. Perhaps you even have a slight smile (at what you're *not* saying).

You've lowered the "fume factor" in yourself and in the room. The calm voice you use when you speak continues to decelerate conflict.

Have fun trying this. You'll thank me later.

Now on to the second tough talk.

Tough Talk #2: This happened with our divorce mediation team. The house had been sold, and our bills as a couple had been paid. Now it was time to create the divorce agreement—especially the financial part.

I had been the primary breadwinner and had set money aside for my retirement. Larry, who already was retired and had not been a planner, had limited funds beyond his half of the money from selling our house.

My goal was to give him my smaller retirement account and keep the larger annuity. My friends told me, "Don't offer him the full amount from the smaller account! Leave yourself some wiggle room, because he'll want to negotiate for more."

My response was, "I don't want to play games about this. I've set a number in my head and that's what I'm sticking to. Because I don't want to pay spousal support."

When we met with our two mediators (one a woman lawyer and the other a male mediator—an approach I recommend), I told everyone what I was willing to do.

Larry responded with, "Isn't Illinois a community property state? Doesn't this mean I'm entitled to *half* of Lynne's retirement?"

That was my biggest fear. I took a deep breath and filled the brown thought cloud with this: "You spent tens of thousands of dollars, lied to hide this from me, and then I paid off all your debts. I can't trust you, which is why this marriage is ending. Now you want to be rewarded with *more* money from me to support you even when we're no longer together!"

This started draining my venom. My pause allowed the mediator to jump in.

"Well, Larry, if a judge saw all of the financial moves you made without Lynne's knowledge or consent, and looked at the amount of money she's willing to give you, I think he'd say this is more than fair."

Larry sighed, then said, "Lynne has always been a fair person, so that's what we'll do."

Those three true things I'd written over a year before set the stage for a parting of the ways, a financial agreement I wanted, and worked for both of us. Now, years later, we are friends, and help and enjoy the other's company. Given the 29 years Larry and I were married, and our shared history, both of us find comfort in that.

Why did I tell you this story? You could say it represents a long form of persuasion.

WHAT IS PERSUASION?

These days, the term "persuasion" has fallen on hard times. Too many people associate it with "manipulation," "control," "making people do things they don't want to," and the mythical smarmy used car salesperson. It's often replaced by "influence." Frankly, I think this is a weasel word designed to feel more politically correct.

Screw that!

Here's *my* definition of persuasion, and the basis for this book:

> ***To present your ideas in a way that people can see them, hear them, and feel them, then decide if what you're proposing is what they are willing to do.***

If so, then to have them say "yes" faster. If not, then to say "no." But you will have built such goodwill in the process that, if they ever need what you offer, they'll reach out to you. Or if they run into someone else who needs this, they'll refer you.

Persuasion isn't about getting everyone to say "yes" to you. It's about helping people make good decisions.

WHY DO YOU NEED PERSUASIONGPS™?

The biggest mistake most of us make when trying new or big-big things (as divorce was for me) is winging it. We say to ourselves, "I've done something like this before, so I know how to handle it." Then we jump in.

Soon the conversation has gone in a direction we didn't—or couldn't—anticipate. Now we're dancing as fast as we can to avoid looking like unprepared idiots. Our focus has shifted to *not looking bad*. That means we're missing opportunities to listen well, connect with others, and adapt to new information—which could result in something better than what we originally proposed.

What if we could apply a system to help us better prepare for—and create more opportunities in—important situations:

- Job interviews
- Salary and job responsibility negotiations
- Board meetings
- Investor presentations
- Strategic planning sessions
- New business presentations
- Client work expansion conversations
- Mergers and acquisitions

- Difficult conversations with board directors or trustees, leaders, supervisors, peers and direct reports
- Tough talks with loved ones

You just saw how writing my three true things resonated throughout a year-long situation. The PersuasionGPS™ approach pulls together all of the strategies and tips I learned and used in ending my marriage—and throughout my career as a communication consultant, persuasion expert, and neuroscience nerd.

You are at your most powerful and persuasive when you know *why* you're here, *what* you want, and *how* to connect with others to make that happen. This book shares all of the best ideas I know for doing that. To make this system easy and usable, here's what "GPS" stands for:

- G = Goals, because magical things happen in your brain and in the world when you set these well
- P = People, not just knowing who they are but how to connect with them based on how their brains work
- S = Showcase, so you clearly present "what's in it for them" in the language they prefer

Pulling these three parts together gives you an easy-to-use framework for fast-tracking your powers of persuasion.

HOW TO GET THE MOST FROM THIS BOOK

This is a slim volume. Even so, don't read it from beginning to end.

Start with the Goals section. Getting clear on these will drive everything else you do—because being fuzzy on where you want to go means it takes you longer to get there (if you ever do). Having meaningful goals will help you choose the best actions to focus on and learn to take in the following chapters.

But don't start at the beginning of each chapter—go to the *end*. The "What You Know" page summarizes everything in that chapter. It gives you an easy outline for what you're about to discover. Now you're ready to dive into the chapter.

Once you're done reading the chapter, turn to the "What to Do Now" pages (after "What You Know"). This is a built-in guidebook. It gives you exercises to integrate the information you just learned and make it your own. That increases the chances you'll actually *use* what you've discovered. (How many books have you read and thought, "Yes, I'll do that!" and never did? Let's take what you're getting here into the real world—so you can benefit from the time and money you've invested.)

TAKE ACTION WITH THE OPEN MINDSET SIGNAL™

As you choose what to use from each chapter, and do the exercises that follow it, here's an approach that will help. The Open Mindset Signal™ is a simple and useful strategy that interrupts your habit of winging it so you can change your thoughts and actions:

- *Stop* before going on autopilot or doing what you've always done. You need to recognize that 1) a situation or relationship is important, 2) your actions have long-lasting implications, or 3) you're striving for a major goal or outcome. This requires a new way of being.
- *Explore* your PersuasionGPS™ tools. Have you set clear and motivating goals? Do you understand the person or people involved in reaching those goals and her/his/their needs, wants, and fears? Do you know the best ways to communicate with that person/those people? Those answers will help you select the most meaningful strategies for connecting with each of them.
- *Go* ahead and implement the more focused approach you created in Explore. Know you've increased the speed and certainty of your chances for success.

To assist with this—and avoid overwhelm—use Chapter 10: Put It All Together. You'll find simple one-page "cheat sheets" with step-by-step actions to apply the information from every chapter.

Now start your journey by identifying and selecting your goals!

PART 1

"G" IS FOR GOALS

Magical Things Happen
in Your Brain and in the World
when You Set Clear Goals

G = GOALS

CHAPTER 1

Find Your Brain

In a crisis, you shut off 2/3rds of your brain,[1] *so you can't make decisions or plan. Know how to turn those parts back on.*

"I'm just so overwhelmed at work!" Gayle said over the phone. "There's so much to do that I can't possibly get it all done—even if I worked 24 hours every day. I can't see how this will ever end!" I could picture her closing her eyes, wrinkling her forehead, and rubbing it with the fingers of her left hand.

My first reaction was to get her to sort through everything on her plate. You know, the practical approach—using the Eisenhower Matrix (developed by that general in World War II).

---

1 Goleman, Daniel. *Emotional Intelligence: Why It Can Matter More Than IQ*. Bantom, 2005.

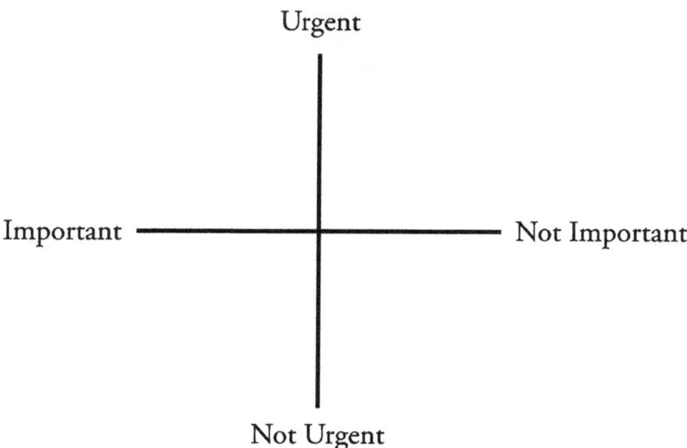

"Let's take all your projects and prioritize them here," I suggested.

"I just have too many to focus on," she replied.

"Why don't we start with doing a list?" I encouraged.

"I already have one," Gayle said.

"Alright, then pull it out."

"No, it's in my head."

"Then how about we write it down as the first step, then figure out where everything goes after that?"

Gayle went silent.

My first—judgmental—reaction was that she was resisting my efforts to get unstuck. Then I realized the fault was mine. None of this was going to help Gayle, because her brain had been hijacked.

This really *does* happen. To know why that is and what to do about it, let's take a quick trip through some practical neuroscience.

OK: I'm a neuroscience nerd. I love studying how the brain works and how that affects our choices and behavior. While I'm as much of a theory wonk as the next person, if I can't put what I learn to work, I don't have too much use for it. Now on to some good stuff you can use.

YOUR THREE BRAINS

There are three parts to your brain.

1. Your ***survival brain*** is the oldest. It's in charge of two things: keeping your body running and keeping you alive. Not a lot of thinking goes on here. You basically have four choices: fight, flight, freeze or fawn (where you bow to someone you believe has more power than you).
2. Your ***emotional brain*** is the place where your feelings live. You generally have five choices here: mad, sad, glad, hurt and afraid—and all the permutations in-between. This also is where you make decisions.
3. Your ***thinking brain*** collects information from your survival and emotional brains—which aren't aware of each other. Its job is to analyze your internal and external data, then develop practical, smart, and ethical plans from which you take action.

These three brains layer on top of each other—and all three are always there.

Triune Brain

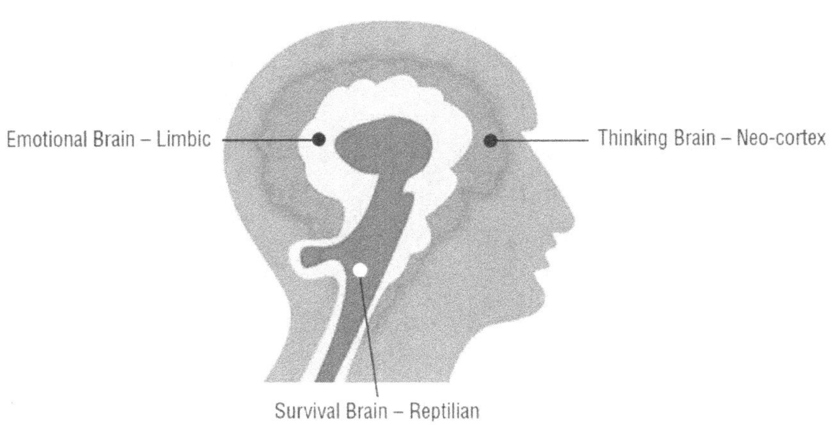

Emotional Brain – Limbic

Thinking Brain – Neo-cortex

Survival Brain – Reptilian

YOUR THREE BRAINS IN CRISIS

In a crisis, you lose access to two-thirds of your brain: your thinking and emotional brains. All you have left is your survival brain. It's logical to wonder why the bulk of your brain would disappear when you need it the most. Here's how I explain this.

Picture the old-old days, when we were living in the jungle. You saw a fast-moving object coming toward you. If your thinking brain were in charge, it would ask, "What *is* this thing coming toward me?" It would analyze the blur. Because "it" happened to be a tiger—*wham!* you'd be dead.

If your emotional brain were in charge, you'd be asking yourself, "How do I *feel* about this thing coming toward me?" And—*wham!* you'd be dead.

Because your survival brain is in charge, it notices the threat before your other two brains do. It already has you up the tree. And—*whew!* you'd be alive.

When you feel frightened or attacked, your body diverts impulses from the thinking and emotional brains to a part of your survival brain, called the amygdala. The amygdala is in charge of scanning your environment for physical and verbal risks and threats. When it perceives these, the amygdala takes over. I love the term for this: "amygdala hijack."

In other words, your amygdala shuts down your other two brains. You lose your emotional intelligence. Stress hormones (epinephrine and cortisol) flood your system. Epinephrine raises your heart rate—so your body can move more blood to the large muscle groups that may need it for fight or flight. It also dilates your pupils—which lets more light into your eyes so you can see better.

Cortisol puts a damper on your immune system, reducing any inflammation you'll suffer if you're wounded. It also gets your brain stem to stimulate your amygdala even more—which, in turn, produces more cortisol. Now there's enough cortisol in your system to suppress your hippocampus—which usually is in charge of putting the brakes on your amygdala. Not surprisingly, your ability to make logical choices drops drastically, and your working memory falters.

You can't reason with someone—including yourself—when you're in amygdala hijack.

That's where Gayle was.

What you need to know now is how to get your brain back.

RECLAIM YOUR BRAIN

While every crisis feels different to you, they all go through the same stages.

The best description I've found to get through this situation comes from psychiatrist Mark Goulston.[2] He calls this the "Oh F#@& to OK" process. Here's a user's guide to get through it.

Reaction Phase ("Oh F#@&")

Back to Gayle. She saw no way out of her crushing workload—*ever*.

"Clients have been promised impossible things, and we don't have the staff to do them," she explained. "So I just keep getting pulled into a worker-bee mode and never get to do the high-level planning and messaging that was supposed to come with my new role. And if I say anything about this, it will confirm to everyone around me that I'm just a big complainer!"

What was going through Gayle's mind was, "Whatever I do, I am screwed. There's no way out!"

How to Get Through It: In her survival brain, Gayle had the four choices of fight, flight, freeze, or fawn. She was stuck in freeze. The

---

2 Goulston, Mark. *Just Listen: Discover the Secret to Getting Through to Absolutely Everyone*. AMACOM 2010.

first thing I *should* have done—and finally did—was ask Gayle to name her feeling.

"I'm afraid I won't be able to do everything they're asking me to. Then they'll fire me. Or I'll have to look for another job. And I just don't have the energy to do *any* of this!"

Gayle didn't know that by saying this, she was taking the first step to reclaiming the next part of her brain. Too often we stay stuck in reaction because we're not willing to admit what we feel. "I'm not afraid," we say to ourselves. Or "I'm not mad." We waste too much energy trying to convince ourselves of something we know deep down isn't true.

Gayle also was holding her breath. I prompted her to do the most calming kind of breathing with me: inhale for a certain number of beats (such as three, which I counted off for her) and exhale for twice that many (six). Knowing that she was in a safe place where no one else would see or interrupt her, I also suggested she close her eyes. This limited her outside stimulation and helped to calm her mind.

Why This Works: There's a helpful line from Dr. Dan Siegel, professor of psychiatry at the UCLA School of Medicine: "Name it to tame it." Once you're not denying your feeling—because you've named it—you start to move into your emotional brain. At least that gets you from four choices to five (mad, sad, glad, hurt, and afraid) and the ability to decide.

Release Phase ("Oh God!")

If you're like me—and Gayle—at this moment you'd love it if someone would come in and save you from whatever mess you're in. During this second phase, you realize that isn't going to happen. But you're still feeling a little victim-y about it.

Gayle said, "We had a new hire quit this week—and we were short-staffed *before* he left. My boss would love to see me fail. Kurt [the company president] already knows about all of these and other issues. But he's in Australia—and what's he going to do about it? I wonder how the heck did I get here?"

Then she said something important. "It's clear no one's going to come to my rescue. I'm going to have to save myself."

How to Get Through It: Gayle needed to vent, and she needed me to listen without interruption or trying to "fix" her situation. She wasn't getting these two things from others in the organization—just the fear that she would be judged and discounted as a complainer.

All I could do was invite her to breathe deeply and keep her eyes closed, to limit some of that information coming through her dilated pupils.

Why This Works: The idea is to take the pause you require to regain your inner balance. You need the chance to calm your body—with all those stress hormones rushing through it. Go ahead: feel a bit sorry for yourself to get this out of your system! Then take the time to get your balance back by continuing to wake up your emotional brain.

Gayle was moving from fear to anger about the lack of support within the company. I encouraged her to talk about this. It was going to give her the energy to make better decisions and, ultimately, act on them when she was ready.

Recenter Phase ("Oh Jeez")

Gayle was feeling beat up and alone. Now it would help if she could calm herself.

How to Get Through It: To support her in moving there, I told Gayle what I often said to myself: "Feelings are *not* facts!" She might *feel* alone, like she didn't have what it took to rise above this, but *that wasn't true.*

I reminded Gayle about how talented, skilled, and resourceful she was. This included specific examples of how I've seen her exhibit these qualities:

- Giving an engaging presentation that won accolades at an industry conference
- Clear-headedly and calmly ending a business partnership with someone who proved to be intractable and nasty
- Being well-respected enough to be elected president of the largest chapter of a national industry association.

That kept my comments from being platitudes and reminded Gayle that she has handled difficult situations before.

As her confidence began to return, I invited her to say, "This is scary, but I can deal with it." I also let her know that she wasn't alone and we were in this together.

Why This Works: I view this as the equivalent of a 12-step program, used by people recovering from addictions. Each action step is preceded by one that *prepares* you to act. For example, Step #8 is "Made a list of all people we had harmed, and became willing to make amends to them all." Then #9 is "Made direct amends to such people wherever possible, except when to do so would injure them or others."

This phase is where you gather your wits and self-assurance, which wakes up your thinking brain. The combination will propel you through the rest of the process.

Refocusing Phase ("Oh Well")

Now you can begin thinking about ways to do damage control and make the best of what's happening. I call it the "getting your righteous indignation to work *for* you" step.

How to Get Through It: Gayle is getting ready to advocate for herself. I invited her to say, "I will *not* let this ruin my day, my career, my relationships with others, my life." Then I asked her to tell me what she needed to do *right now* to make things better.

The "right now" is important. If you're like me, you can project yourself so far into the future that you miss the present. Earlier, Gayle talked about getting fired or quitting because she needed to find a different job. Looking way down the line can paralyze you. It can make the problem so big that you feel overwhelmed—not a good choice in this moment! Stick with what you need to get through the next 15 minutes or hour, rather than the next day, week, or month. There will be time to figure out the other stuff later.

Why It Works: Because you've gone through the other three phases, you now have your thinking brain back. This means you are physiologically able to start considering what you *can* do to limit what's going wrong and make the best of the situation you face.

In Gayle's case, she knew she had dealt with difficult times before. She was back in touch with the confidence in her abilities to handle these.

Reengaging Phase ("OK")

Gayle was able to identify the projects she needed to get done *today*. She also had a standing call with Kurt (the company president) this afternoon. Now she was ready to strategize what to do next.

How to Get Through It: You have reached the point where you can say to yourself, "I'm ready to handle this." And you'll be right. If you've had your eyes closed while working through the other phases, you can open them and see more than disaster. Now you can understand why the Chinese character for the word "crisis" is the combination of two others: "danger" and "opportunity." You see beyond catastrophe to better things.

Gayle started looking at each of the activities she was able to do that day, and how she would move them forward. She also was deciding what to say to those who want something *now* and won't get it from her, and the best way to communicate that.

Next, we discussed what she needed to say to Kurt about what was happening. Gayle briefly fell back into "Oh God." She said, "He already knows about all of these issues and will be tired of hearing about them from me again." I could hear her confidence slipping. She was losing "opportunity" and falling back into "danger."

It's not unusual to bounce around among the phases—so there's no judgment. The choice we need to make is not to *stay* there.

"How can we make this conversation different from the ones you've had before?" I asked. Gayle now had the brainpower to answer.

We discussed specific examples of how putting her in the position of "worker-bee" prevented Gayle from doing the things Kurt wanted: adding revenue and profit to the company. She decided to ask him what *he* thought they should do to deal with the situation (to give Kurt a personal stake in what was happening). She also would suggest they hire not just one person to replace the employee who left, but two—to leverage the hiring and onboarding process, and give the company a needed cushion if one of those people didn't work out.

Why It Works: You have allowed your brain to go through all of the stages it needs to recover from amygdala hijack. Plus you have done this without short-changing yourself emotionally, which would have happened if you had denied your feelings and pretended that you weren't hurt, or sad, or angry. Or afraid, which is where Gayle had been. (I'm betting you won't lose your mind because you're so happy. However, you could make some poor choices when your brain is flooded with endorphins or dopamine!)

By working through the Reengaging Phase, you emerge with a thoughtful plan for what to do now—rather than grabbing hold of the first idea you come across and hoping it will work. You also come out with a better sense of your own worth and the chance to show this to others.

NOW YOU KNOW HOW TO GET YOUR BRAIN—OR SOMEONE ELSE'S—BACK

Often we go through crises because we're focused on how the world *should* be, but *isn't*—and probably never will be. Gayle thought there was no way to get out of the hole she was in, so she could only give up and get fired or leave. The process of getting our brains back prepares us to deal with the world as it *is*.

It may take a while to train your brain to pass through all of these steps—because, after all, you've lost your mind! But with practice, you can reduce the amount of time it takes to move through this process. The Open Mindset Signal™—Stop/Explore/Go—is a good place to begin.

Some people can travel through all these stages in only a few minutes. But if you've been stuck in one of the phases before—the "why does this happen to me?" victimhood of the Release Phase has been a traditional favorite of mine—you now know how you may move past it.

Just as important is the knowledge that your family, friends, clients, and even the stranger who cuts you off on the highway can be doing this because *they* are going through amygdala hijack.

When people are stuck in the Reaction Phase, you may see all kinds of aggression they use to mask their fear, hurt, and sadness. Often this shows up as strident, vein-pulsing anger, because they are literally scared out of *their* minds. Other people may react with tears, or silence.

Now you know they are in their survival brains. It may be your job—or your gift to them—to help them get *their* brains back. It all starts with that simple question, "What are you feeling?"

If I had been wise enough to ask that of Gayle right away—rather than trying to "fix" her situation by asking her to make a prioritized list—it would have saved some flailing around.

WHAT YOU KNOW

- You have three brains:
  1. Your survival brain keeps your body running and alive. You have four options here: fight, flight, freeze, or fawn.
  2. Your emotional brain contains all of your feelings. You have five options here—mad, sad, glad, hurt, and afraid—plus decision-making.
  3. Your thinking brain houses all of your higher analytical powers and normally is aware of your other two brains.

- You lose access to two-thirds of your mind when in crisis. All you have left is your survival brain. The part of it that's in charge is called the amygdala. It overrides everything else when it senses a physical or verbal threat.

- You can get your brain back by following Mark Goulston's "Oh F#@& to OK" process:
  a. ***Reaction Phase:*** You think all is lost and your only options are fight, flight, freeze, or fawn. Start waking up your emotional brain by asking, "What am I feeling?"
  b. ***Release Phase:*** You wish someone would rescue you but understand this won't happen. Breathe deeply and admit that you're going to have to do this yourself.
  c. ***Recenter Phase:*** Keep breathing and know that you have the resources to deal with this. Now you're starting to get your thinking brain back.
  d. ***Refocus Phase:*** This is where you combine your emotional and thinking brains, using anger on your own behalf by saying to yourself, "I'm not going to let this ruin my life!"
  e. ***Reengaging Phase:*** Your thinking brain is back. You're ready to strategize on what to do *now* to deal with this.

WHAT TO DO NOW

Learn from Your Past

1. Remember a chaotic situation when it felt as though you had lost your mind (in the Open Mindset Signal™, this is ***Stop***):

   a. Where and when did this take place?

   ____

   ____

   b. What happened?

   ____

   ____

   c. What were you doing?

   ____

   ____

   d. Who else was involved?

   ____

   ____

2. Now consider what you would do differently if this happened today, and you applied the five phases of getting your brain back (in the Open Mindset Signal™, this is ***Explore***):

   a. Reaction Phase – how would you get past "I'm screwed!"?

   ____

   ____

   b. Release Phase – how do you move beyond your wish to be rescued?

   ____

   ____

   c. Recenter Phase – what resources do you have to handle this situation?

   ____

   ____

   d. Refocus Phase – what won't you let this situation ruin for you?

   ____

   ____

e. Reengaging Phase – what will you do to start making things better in the next few minutes? (*Go* in the Open Mindset Signal™.)

____

____

3. How is this different from what actually happened?

____

____

Prepare for the Future Exercise

1. List some events you are afraid might escalate into a crisis.

____

____

2. Close your eyes and place yourself in one of those situations.
3. Ask yourself, "What am I feeling?"
4. What will you do after this?

____

____

G = GOALS

CHAPTER 2

Use Your Brain for Goals

Your brain already is helping and hindering you with reaching your goals. Know how to amplify the useful stuff and dump the rest.

Jennifer said, "I finally found my dream job, and I'm going to have to quit." I could hear the exasperation in her clipped tone over the phone and pictured the eye roll accompanying it.

What made the job ideal? It was with a startup, which developed an integrated marketing platform for a professional services industry. Nothing else on the market offered all its features and functions. Jennifer was a true believer in how this product would strip time and complexity from marketing while using data to improve decision-making. She also had an equity position in the company, which would pay off when another firm purchased it.

Why did she need to quit? She wasn't even making subsistence-level compensation, since the key performance indicators (KPIs) created for her bonus weren't based in reality. Her supervisor, Bob, was a controlling bully. He would praise her in front of others, then demean and undermine her confidence when they were one-on-one. Bob also blocked her access to the company president (Michael), senior leaders, and the data she needed to do her job.

Two weeks before, it appeared Jennifer had made a breakthrough. She arranged a Zoom meeting with Bob and Michael. We created three goals for this negotiation:

1. Pay the target number she set for compensation
2. Remove her from Bob's team so she reports directly to Michael
3. Include her in senior leadership meetings and give her access to the data everyone else receives

While Bob contested much of this, Michael agreed to Jennifer's requests. It appeared all of her goals had been met! Then Michael stopped returning her messages. Bob told her she would *still* have to report to him, and snickered about how he'd come up with new KPIs and rules for her.

Now you know why she wanted to quit! Jennifer had seen some initial success, then everything seemed to go back to what it was. She thought there was no hope for improvement.

GOALS AND THE "NEGATIVE" BRAIN

Here's a good definition of a goal: "a result you can attain but will require intentional action and often cooperation with others to get there." What Jennifer created fits that description.

She pursued her three goals for that conversation and seemed to reach them. Then a breakdown occurred, which had nothing to do with what she said or did. Now she thought all was lost, and she needed to get out. Why did that seem the most viable option?

Our Brains Are Designed to Be Negative: In the last chapter, we discussed how our brains were originally designed to keep us alive. They search for risks and threats, then get us out of the way.

Our subconscious mind is still doing that today. It's looking for things that could go wrong and urging us to avoid them. This means we're much better at spotting the bad than watching for opportunities for good stuff.

Our Brains Live in the Past: They default to what either prevented pain or created good results for us so far. Then they prompt us to keep doing that—whether or not the current situation warrants it. And that's because …

Our Brains Are Lazy: Most big goals take sustained activity. Lisa Feldman Barrett is a University Distinguished Professor at Northeastern University. She explains that our brain's primary job is to allocate energy to the areas of our bodies and to activities that will keep us alive.[3] (Even in a resting state, the average adult brain consumes 20% of the body's energy.) As a result, our brains don't want to think too hard unless there's a proven reward (or avoidance of risk) in this. Our brains would rather take shortcuts (not think too hard) to conserve energy in case something else more important comes up.

Jennifer was feeling the effects of all three factors. She'd labored under poor compensation and leadership for nine months and was having trouble imagining this would ever end. She thought Michael had been on her side before, but then he disappeared, leaving her at

---

3 Barrett, Lisa Feldman, *7-1/2 Lessons about the Brain*, Houghton Mifflin Harcourt, 2020.

Bob's mercy. She was tired of trying to find other ways to get what she wanted. Jennifer felt it was time to get a new job—even if the new position was less than ideal.

How could I help Jennifer move beyond the negative stuff going on in her brain (some genetic, some situational) to get her what she wanted?

"Let's give it one more shot." I said.

USE GOALS TO LEVERAGE AND REWIRE THE BRAIN

Yes: the brain is wired to focus on the negative and seek safety by avoiding risks. That doesn't mean we are stuck there. Now it's time to play with your brain!

You know you have three brains (page 3). You also have two minds. What's the difference? I like the definition from Rick Hanson, senior fellow at University of California Berkeley's Greater Good Science Center: "The mind *is* what the brain *does*."[4] (The italics are mine.) These are your conscious and subconscious minds. This graphic offers a helpful distinction.

---

4 Hanson, Rick; Mendius, Richard. *Buddha's Brain*. New Harbinger Publications, Inc. 2009.

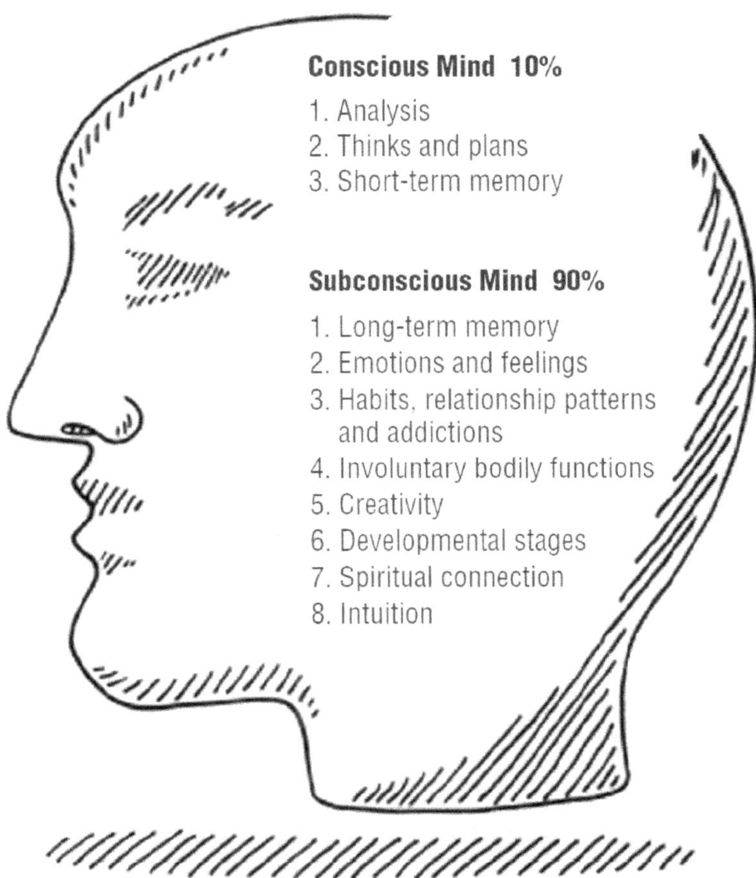

As you can see, your conscious mind is your thinking brain. You know what's going on here—and now you know how little that is in the larger playground in your head! Your subconscious is part of your emotional and survival brains—which, once again, coexist but aren't aware of each other.

While we don't know a lot about what's going on in our subconscious mind, we do know two things: 1) it wants us to get what we want, and 2) we have to tell it what that is.

Get Your Conscious and Subconscious Minds Working with *You:* Your conscious mind can process between 10 to 50 bits of data per second. As the next table shows, your senses are transmitting way more than that—just from what's going on *outside* your body[5]:

Sensory System	Bits of Information per Second
Eyes	10 million
Skin	1 million
Ears	100,000
Smell	100,000
Taste	1,000

Your subconscious mind handles 11+ million bits of information per second! That means it has access to a lot more than you know you have.

This is where your reticular activating system (RAS) comes in. It is the bridge between your conscious and subconscious minds. It's the pathway that nearly all information uses to get into your brain. (The one exception is smells. These go directly to your emotional brain.) The RAS filters all the information that enters your brain and determines what you pay attention to—and what you screen out.

Biologically speaking, the RAS is a loose confederation of nuclei in your brain stem—part of your survival brain. There are two sections in the RAS: ascending and descending. The first connects with the thinking brain, as well as the thalamus and hypothalamus. The second links to the cerebellum and the other four senses. This means the RAS also plays an important role in breathing, sleeping, waking, and your heartbeat.

As a gatekeeper, the RAS is more active during the day than at night. What does this have to do with getting clear on your goals? You can't do it without the RAS.

---

5 Encyclopedia Britannica, Applications of Information Theory, Physiology. Viewed at https://www.britannica.com/science/information-theory/Physiology on April 18, 2025.

If I told you, "Don't think about a red corvette," what are you thinking about? Right! That's because—suddenly—your RAS understands that a red corvette is important to you. For the rest of this week, you probably will be surprised by the number of red corvettes you see. While they were there all along, your RAS didn't know these cars were worth noticing, so it didn't bring them to your attention.

Chances are that you have experienced your RAS in other ways, too. Let's say that you're an Alfred Hitchcock film buff. Last night you watched one of your favorites: "North by Northwest." Tonight, you're at a networking event with other business leaders. The room is filled with conversations. You're enjoying one with the head of human resources at a health care company. From behind you, you hear, "I'm trying to remember who played the villain in that movie 'North by Northwest.'" You turn around and say, "That was James Mason." Then you return to your conversation.

How did you happen to hear *that* question among all of the buzz in this room? It's because your RAS was already tuned in to that movie title, so when someone said it, the RAS let it through to your conscious mind.

Your RAS responds to two types of information: novelty and repetition. We're particularly interested in the latter.

Setting goals—whether short-term about a meeting or longer term about your career—gets your conscious and subconscious minds working together to help you get what you want. You literally have to tell your RAS what this is—by writing or speaking your goals, and repeating them. Then it goes to work, monitoring those millions of bits of data per second to find the people, articles, YouTube videos, and other resources that will help you get there. And—miraculously—all of these start showing up in your life!

Maybe this has happened to you, too. I've gone to bed thinking about an issue or asking myself a question: "What can I do to get that potential client—who has been sitting on my proposal for two weeks—to work with me?"

Often I'll wake up in the middle of the night, or the next morning, with an answer or strategy to use. "I'll call the client and say, 'Something is preventing you from saying yes to working with me. If you tell me what it is, I'll try to find a way to get you what you need, so you can make a good decision.'" That's because my RAS and subconscious have been "chewing" on it while I was sleeping. These ideas always feel like such a gift!

Here's the important thing to remember about the RAS. It can't tell the difference between a *positive* and a *negative* message. This is best embodied by a quote often attributed to the pioneering car maker Henry Ford: "Whether you think you can or you think you can't, you're right."

Have you ever struggled with a proposal or presentation and thought, "They'll *never* sign off on this idea!" Guess what? Your RAS heard "never sign off on this idea" and is working hard to make sure you use words, tactics and strategies so that happens. Be *careful* what you feed your RAS!

Your RAS and Goal Setting: Whether or not you believe in the law of attraction, your RAS does.

It turns out that the Harvard 1979 and Yale 1953 studies of the importance of written goals were both urban myths. However, Dominican University took up the gauntlet in 2013.[6]

Dr. Gail Matthews did a month-long goal study, which was completed by 149 people. They ranged in age from 23 to 72, with 37 men and 112 women. Participants came from Australia,

---

6 Tabaka, Marla, "New Study Says This Simple Step Will Increase the Odds of Achieving Your Goals (Substantially)," January 28, 2019, *Inc. Magazine*. Viewed at https://www.inc.com/marla-tabaka/this-study-found-1-simple-step-to-practically-guarantee-youll-achieve-your-goals-for-real.html on April 18, 2025.

Belgium, England, India, Japan and the U.S. Their professions included entrepreneurs, educators, healthcare professionals, artists, attorneys, bankers, marketers, human services providers, managers, vice presidents and directors of not-for-profits.

These people were divided into five groups:

1. ***Group 1:*** Thought about a goal and then rated it on these dimensions: a) difficulty, b) importance, c) the extent to which they had the skills and resources to accomplish the goal, d) their commitment and motivation to reach the goal, e) whether or not they had pursued this goal in the past, and f) their level of success if they had worked toward the goal before
2. ***Group 2:*** Same as Group 1 but also wrote the goal (into an online survey)
3. ***Group 3:*** Same as Group 2 but also developed action commitments to reach the goal
4. ***Group 4:*** Same as Group 3 but also sent their goals and action commitments to a supportive friend
5. ***Group 5:*** Same as Group 4 but also sent weekly progress reports to a supportive friend

Just *thinking* about their goals helped 43% of the people in Group 1 achieve them. I say that's a strong vote for the RAS! Of course the other groups did better, with Group 2 at 61%, Group 3 at 51%, Group 4 at 64% and Group 5 at 76%.

Rewiring Jennifer's Brain: Remember Jennifer thinking she couldn't have her ideal job? She believed there were no possible positive outcomes here. So her subconscious mind kept sending up information and actions (such as "time to find a new job") to support that view.

To get her beyond this, I asked, "Don't you have a Zoom meeting with Michael this afternoon?"

"Yes—if he shows up," she snarked. (She was justified. Michael occasionally flaked on these sessions.)

"What would you like to say to him if he *does* come?"

She sighed. "He's heard this all before. He'll just think I'm complaining."

"Forget about him," I replied. "What would *you* like to say for *yourself*?"

"I'd like to tell him all the wonderful things I could do in this job if they'd just give me the resources, pay, and freedom to do them!"

We dug deeply into what these would be. Jennifer started getting excited about how this would look.

Then we created an agenda for what she'd like to discuss. She sent it to Michael in advance as a prompt to remind him to come.

When he arrived, Jennifer focused on the two things she wanted him to know. First, that she'd taken an idea he mentioned about a new product earlier in the week and already scheduled a call with a prospect to get reactions to it. Second, that she had another idea for expanding relationships with existing clients.

Michael was shocked! "You mean you took something I said in passing two days ago and already are moving forward with it?"

"Of course," Jennifer said. "I know this person well, and he's the ideal guy to give us feedback on your idea."

Michael shook his head in disbelief at Jennifer's speed. He also was impressed with her existing client idea. Now it was easy for Jennifer to make her ask.

"By the way, I haven't heard anything about the topics we discussed two weeks ago: one, my compensation; two, moving out of Bob's group; and three, becoming a part of the leadership meetings and getting access to data. Could you tell me what's happening?"

Michael confirmed that all of this was in the works, and that he'd have the chief of staff contact her the next week with the details. Yes: that did happen!

Jennifer went from being grossly underpaid to the highest-paid person in the company—even more than Michael and Bob. She got everything else she asked for, too. She was able to do this for two reasons. First, she shifted her negative mindset, and second, she created messages that showcased her value to Michael so he saw—and wanted—what Jennifer would bring.

Imagine how powerful this could be in *your* daily life. You can't expect your RAS to take you where you want to go unless you're clear on what that is, let alone where it could take the people you lead.

Start with the small stuff. What do you want to get out of your next meeting? Your next phone conversation? Your next email? That difficult conversation you've been putting off with your spouse or child?

I can't promise you'll become the highest-paid person at *your* organization. But I can say you'll get your conscious and subconscious minds working together to get what you want. Not only will you stop falling short of what's possible for you, but you'll also show others how valuable you are—at home and in the office!

WHAT YOU KNOW

- Our brains can sabotage us in three ways, and we don't even know it:
  1. They are designed to be negative—looking for risks and threats (even ones that aren't there) and doing what they can to keep us safe.
  2. They live in the past—defaulting to what's worked before, because this seems less risky.
  3. They are lazy—wanting to conserve energy for other tasks and not wanting to think too hard on this one (unless we let them know this *is* important).

- Your conscious mind processes 10–50 bits of information per second and accounts for about 10% of your mental activity (analyzing, thinking and planning, and short-term memory). Your subconscious mind houses everything else.

- Your reticular activating system (RAS) is the literal bridge between your conscious and subconscious minds. It sifts through the 11 million+ bits of information your brain captures every second and brings the relevant ones to your attention. This makes it important in setting goals.

- Your subconscious mind wants you to get what you want, but you literally have to tell it. At the same time, your subconscious mind can't discriminate between positive and negative messages, so be careful what you focus on.

WHAT TO DO NOW

Conundrum-Breaking Goal Setting Exercise

1. Before going to bed tonight, think of a problem that has been concerning or troubling you. (In the Open Mindset Signal™, this is ***Stop***.)
2. Close your eyes and take a deep breath.
3. Ask yourself, "What can I do tomorrow that will help me with this [problem]?" (***Explore*** in the Open Mindset Signal™.)
4. Or say to yourself, "I want to [state your goal]. Help me find ways to do this."
5. Take another deep breath, then relax and go to sleep.
6. The next morning—or if you wake up in the middle of the night—record any ideas that come to you.
7. Determine which ones you want to try. Note how successful they are. (***Go*** in the Open Mindset Signal™.)

Changing Your Negative Mind Exercise

Your brain defaults to a negative view, because it looks for risks, defaults to what's worked before, and is lazy. This causes automatic negative thoughts (ANTs), which can be conscious or subconscious. They show up involuntarily in response to everyday events. These thoughts are irrational, self-defeating, and come from negative beliefs we have about ourselves. We have about 70,000 thoughts per day: 80% of them are negative and, of those, 95% are repetitive.)

1. Start by noticing your negative thoughts—you can only change them if you know what they are. (One of Jennifer's was, "I can't have my ideal job.") (***Stop***)

2. Write down a negative thought when it shows up:

____

____

3. Dig deeper by answering some questions (***Explore***):

    a. What situation triggered the thought?

    ____

    ____

    b. What facts support the truth of this thought?

    ____

    ____

    c. What evidence/experience disproves it?

    ____

    ____

    d. What have I done before when this thought has cropped up? What happened when I did that?

    ____

    ____

e. How would my life change if I no longer believed this thought?

f. What would I say to a good friend who said she/he/they had this thought?

g. What positive thought do I want to replace this with? (***Go***)

h. How does that positive thought make me feel *now?*

G = GOALS

CHAPTER 3

Create Goals to Motivate Your Brain

Magic things happen in your brain—and in your world—when you set goals well.

It was the call you hate to get.

John was the new CEO of a public company that made industrial valves. I'd written the first draft of his annual shareholders' letter. We were scheduled to meet on Monday morning to discuss it. As I was getting ready to leave for this, his assistant Rachel called.

"We need to push your 10:00 meeting to 3:00 this afternoon," she said. "John was supposed to fly back last night, but the weather was so bad that they cancelled his flight, so he's coming in this morning."

"No problem," I replied. "That time works for me."

"John went to Cape Cod," Rachel explained. "He was planning to relax on his sailboat. But it was windy and rainy all weekend, so he was stuck inside the whole time."

She paused, then added, "I've never heard him in such a foul mood. He said he wants to *torch* your shareholders' letter copy."

That's a meeting I really want to go to! And now I have six hours to obsess about how awful it was going to be.

My default approach would have been to have a low-grade sense of dread in the back of my head all day. I would have tried to soothe myself by saying, "I've handled clients in a bad mood before, so I certainly can deal with John." Then I would have proceeded to go into the meeting and wing it.

Chances are good it would have gone something like this:

"Hi John. I was sorry to hear the lousy weather kept you inside all weekend."

"That's not the only thing that's lousy. This shareholders' letter is the worst thing I've ever read! It's nothing like what I told you I wanted to say. What you wrote is terrible and I'm not going to pay you anything for this."

If you remember the first chapter, you've probably identified that I was in amygdala hijack—shutting down everything except fight, flight, freeze, or fawn. (I likely would have gone into "freeze.") On top of being defensive, I'd be worried about getting paid! I would likely spend all of my energy tap dancing around what to say next. That means I probably wouldn't hear everything John has to say, which would further infuriate him. This drastically reduced the chances that anything would turn out well for *either* of us.

As you may recall from the second chapter, the picture of this unpleasant future would now be coursing from my conscious to my subconscious brain, through the reticular activating system (RAS). That means my subconscious mind is looking for ways to make this rotten situation a reality!

How do we break this death spiral?

I believe the answer is setting goals and finding ways to reach them.

GOALS, WISHES, EXPECTATIONS, AND RESOLUTIONS

Remember our definition of a *goal* as "a result you can attain but will require intentional action and often cooperation with others to get there"? Often we confuse this with three other ideas that are unhelpful substitutes.

The first is a *wish*: "a desire or hope that something could happen." Or even worse: "to want something that cannot or probably will not happen."

I could have spent a few hours *wishing* that John would be in a better mood by the time we met. (Considering that he'd have spent time in airports and a plane before then, it's hard to imagine that experience would lift his spirits.) Or I could wish that his plane would go down—and he'd come away from this harrowing experience with a new perspective and greater appreciation for my work.

You get where this is going. In this instance, a wish would focus on someone other than me, who suddenly—and magically—changes. It's basically me crossing my fingers. *That* rarely works.

Next, we have *expectations*: "a strong belief that something will happen or be the case in the future." This appears to be a wish on steroids. I could *expect* John to see the value of my ideas for his shareholders' letter once we're together, but that doesn't mean he *will*. (How many times have we come out of a meeting with unmet expectations?)

Then there are *resolutions*: "a firm decision to do or not to do something." This is more active than a wish. However, research on New Year's resolutions shows that we're generally lame when it comes to these:[7]

---

7 HQ Hire, "22 Goal-Setting Statistics You Should Know in 2025 (Facts and Studies)." Viewed at https://hqhire.com/goal-setting-statistics/ on April 18, 2025.

- 44% of Americans (12–18% of people worldwide) set New Year's resolutions
- 23% of all New Year's resolutions will be given up within a week, followed by 36% at two weeks, 50% at three months, and 54% at six months
- Only 9% of people will set and achieve their resolutions

I could *resolve* that I wouldn't let John be nasty to me just because he'd had a bad weekend (when *his* expectations of sailing weren't met). But research indicates that's not enough.

Here are the two factors that prevent wishes, expectations, and resolutions from becoming goals that motivate us.

They're Not Realistic or Attainable: "Hopes," "beliefs" and "decisions" often are based on magical thinking:

- The entrepreneur who *wants* to double the size of his business this year
- The leader who *believes* the team should follow her without question
- The CEO who *decides* to take the company into a totally new market

Daydreaming is a wonderful way to expand beyond the usual options that come up when we're considering something. But when there's no relation to what's truly *possible*, goals that are too big become a *disincentive*. We get discouraged and quit. And, along the way, we may blame others, or shame them, or find ways to justify ourselves. That makes it even harder to get the cooperation we need from people to reach good goals when we set these.

They're Vague: That's what happened in the three bullet points above. What does "double the size of the business" mean to the entrepreneur? What happens to the business when no one ever questions the leader? How will the CEO know when the company has successfully entered the new market?

This also makes it hard to track our progress. Unless we have a clear definition—which is part of what makes a good goal—we won't know when we've achieved something.

Now that we know what *doesn't* work, here's an easy system to avoid those pitfalls.

STEP #1: CREATE YOUR *COMMUNICATION GOAL*

I'll admit a bias upfront. My mission statement is *to use communication to help people solve their problems and get what they want.* That's the lens through which I view creating goals.

This means I begin by developing an overarching *communication goal*: that's the result I want from whatever I'm saying or doing.

Setting a communication goal allows you to do two valuable things before you speak with or write to anyone. First, it gets you out of the "negative brain" trap by having you focus on a positive outcome. Second, it moves your focus beyond yourself, which makes whatever you're doing more likely to appeal to others and get their buy-in. (How many times have you heard people blather on about something that has everything to do with *them* and nothing to do with *you*? Don't be that person!)

A useful place to start is knowing the five basic functions of business communication:

a. *Inform*—to share information
b. *Request*—ask for something
c. *Record*—tell people about a meeting or event that has already happened
d. *Instruct*—tell people how to do something
e. *Persuade*—get people to do something

With a clear "what," you can move into the "why." You do this by answering two simple but powerful questions:

1. What's my point?
2. Why does it matter?

Write your communication goal based on your answers. Here's what I came up with for the meeting I was dreading with John:

Persuade John to give me the feedback I need to create a letter that 1) gives shareholders the information they need, and 2) showcases John as a strong new president.

STEP #2: BRAINSTORM YOUR *ACTION GOALS*

Too often people skip Step #1 and jump right into the "how." However, having your communication goal makes the second step easier.

You'll be glad to know this will only take about five minutes. And it will be very effective—because *how* you do it will be based on how *your* brain works.

Freewriting

Use this approach if you're more of a right-brained and creative sort.

Grab a blank sheet of paper (lined or unlined—your choice) and a pen. Set a timer for five minutes. Think about what you want to see happen, then write without stopping. All you want to do is get the ideas out of your head. Use these principles of brainstorming:

1. Don't censor yourself: write everything that occurs to you, no matter how far-fetched it appears.

2. Don't pay attention to grammar, spelling, punctuation, word choice, sentences—anything but your goals.
3. When the timer goes off, stop writing.

Mind Mapping

If you're more of an analytical, logical thinker, this is a better choice.

Again, you need a blank sheet of paper and a pen, and a timer set for five minutes. Not surprisingly, the approach is a little more structured:

1. Pick a phrase that represents the main issue (mine would have been "Productive Meeting with John"). Write it in the center of the page. Then draw a circle around it.
2. Brainstorm without considering if something is a "good" or a "bad" idea. Write a short phrase that represents each (one of mine would have been "we improve the letter"). Then circle it and draw a line back to the main issue in the middle of the page.
3. When the timer sounds, stop.

Most of the time, you'll be amazed by the number of ideas you can generate so quickly using either approach!

Why This Works

In both approaches, thinking about *ideas* and *words* stimulates your *left brain*. The physical activity of *writing* (words in freewriting, plus the circles and lines in mind mapping) excites your *right brain*. This means your entire brain is involved in problem solving!

Avoid any predilection for doing this on your computer or using mind mapping software programs. In this instance, the low-tech approach of writing by hand better serves you. As a species, we've been writing by hand for longer than we've been typing. We need the feel of holding a pen and the arm movement across a page (or holding a stylus and skittering it across a tablet) to engage our right brains. Sitting at the computer gives you minimal arm motion, just your fingers, really. This isn't enough to engage your right brain, so typing out words leads to a disproportionate influence from your left brain.

There's also something very freeing and childlike about 1) writing without using grammar and punctuation, or 2) making big scrawls without worrying how they look as you do them!

The five-minute limit really works. It's enough time to get the most important points out of your head. I've found much of what I come up with after that is repetitious or doesn't add a lot. My time is better spent organizing the good stuff I've already come up with.

For my meeting with John, I used mind mapping. Here is a reconstruction of what I wrote.

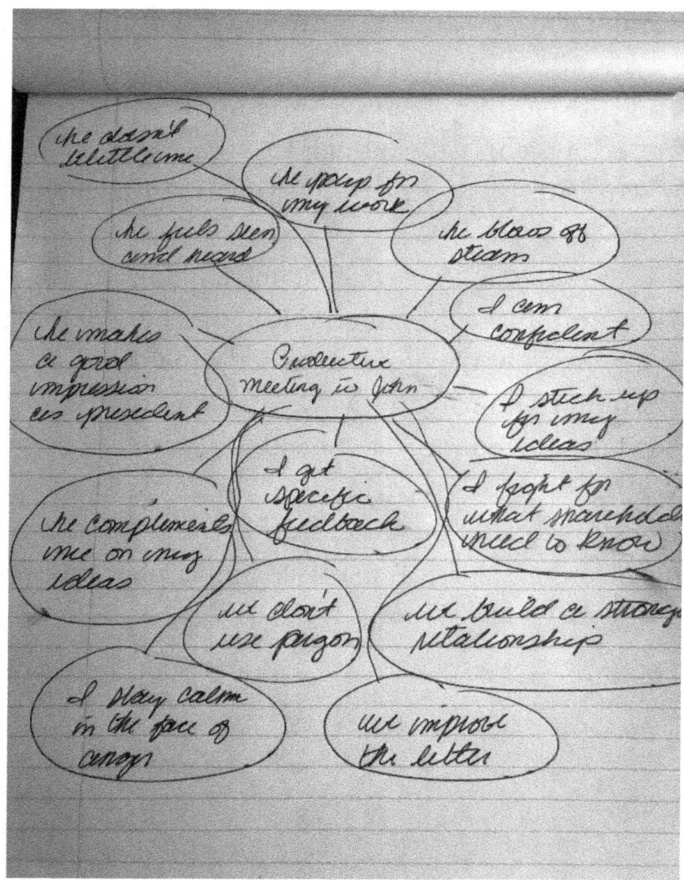

STEP #3: PICK YOUR THREE GOALS

I call it the ***Rule of Three Ideas.*** Your short-term memory can only hold three ideas (and three subpoints for each) before it gets full.

You've just come up with a long list of all the goals you can have to deal with a person or situation. To say, "I'm going to do each of these!" is to set yourself up for failure. First, you won't remember all of them. Second, your efforts will become too scattered. In an attempt to do too much, chances are you'll make a bit of progress on a lot of things and not complete anything.

Use this step to help you focus.

For Both: Go back and read what you wrote. It's normal that not everything is useful. Plenty of times you might have been writing things just to keep your hand going. That was great, because it likely spurred other ideas.

For Freewriting: Look over everything you've written.

1. When you see an idea that stands out, call it out: circle it (with a different color pen), highlight it, or choose your own approach that makes it easy to find.
2. Review everything you've flagged, and pick the three most important goals.

For Mind Mapping: Now you have your best thoughts on one easy-to-read sheet. You also have a few clinkers, which you wrote so you could keep your mind and hand in motion.

1. Put a big red "X" through the ones that are off-target, unimportant, or just silly. (One from my mind map that got tossed was "he compliments me on my ideas.")
2. Look at each remaining phrase. Think about how important or relevant it is. Then place a number above it that represents this, starting at "1" for the most important.
3. Now you easily prioritized your top three goals.

Instead of spending the next few hours fretting—and probably not getting any other work done—these were the three goals I selected for a productive meeting with John:

1. Let him blow off steam: *so he's not dumping negative energy from somewhere else into our meeting*

2. Advocate for shareholders: *because we must share what they need to know, and doing this would show John is a good leader*
3. Get actionable feedback: *because comments like "I don't like the flow" are impossible to address*

I wrote these on a clean sheet of paper—beneath my communication goal. This was my plan. I'd place the sheet on the passenger seat as I drove to the meeting, looking at it while waiting at each stoplight. Arriving in the parking lot, I'd sit in the car, close my eyes, then say the three goals out loud to myself before entering the building.

Heading out the door of my office, I looked at a shelf above my desk. Sitting on it was a polished brass blowtorch. A friend had purchased it for me years ago, because I was fond of saying, "The only way my desk will *ever* be clear is if I use a blowtorch on it!" (There have been times of great disarray when I have taken it down, pointed it at my desk, and made blowtorch combustion sounds.)

I decided to take a risk. When John walked through the conference room door, his expression was every bit as stormy as the weather had been for him that weekend. The sheaf of marked up shareholders' letter pages was slightly crumpled and clutched in his left hand.

"Hi John," I said, rising. "Rachel told me that you felt like 'torching this letter.' As your consultant, it's my job to help you get what you want. Here you go. Torch away!" I held the blowtorch out to him.

John glowered at the blowtorch. For a few seconds, I wasn't sure which way this was going. Then a slow smile spread across his face. John put down the papers and took the blowtorch.

He told me how he had bought an old wooden-bottomed sailboat. John spent the summer renovating it. This included using a blowtorch to remove barnacles and old varnish on the hull, so he could sand, re-stain, and varnish it. Then he showed me the proper way to light and hold the torch.

John relaxed. After saying, "This is a really nice blowtorch!" he was ready to move on to the text.

Here's the funny thing. John's changes were relatively minor. I left the meeting with a clear direction on his revisions. This allowed me to incorporate his comments while showing shareholders he understood their needs and was addressing these. John left the meeting having relived a pleasant memory with an attentive audience and feeling better about me as someone who listened to him (meeting a goal that hadn't made my top three: creating a stronger relationship). All because I had taken a few minutes to write my goals—and was able to notice that blowtorch on the shelf to meet the *first* one!

STEP #4: HAVE A PLAN AND TRACK YOUR PROGRESS

With a clear communication goal, backed by three action goals, you're ready to create the plan to make it all happen. People with written goals increase their chances of achieving them by 42%. Those with a concrete plan are 10-times more likely to be successful.[8] This also includes being prepared if things go sideways.

Allow for Breakdowns: Yes: crap happens. Remember those unattainable and unrealistic goals from earlier in this chapter? The entrepreneur doesn't double the size of his business because the company becomes embroiled in a lawsuit. The leader's best employees don't like following her without question—and leave. The CEO's competitors in the new market cut their prices so the company's plans to expand here never get out of the red.

---

8 Op. cit. HQ Hire.

Spend time thinking about the scenarios that could prevent you from getting what you want. Figure out what you'll do if they happen. Then if they do, you'll be ready to act quickly—rather than losing time to "poor me"s and giving up.

Celebrate Your Progress. Too often we wait until the end (if we celebrate at all). As you reach milestones, reward yourself. Share your successes with people who are important to you. Recognize those working at your side with a little gift (find out in advance what they like!). These things help retrain our brains to adopt new behavior—plus they add some fun to a longer term effort.

CHANGING THE AWFUL TRUTH

Left to its own devices, your brain will keep doing what it thinks has worked before—or at least not failed miserably—because this feels safe. But I want *more* for you (and you do, too).

Skip the wishes, expectations, and resolutions. Set goals that are specific, and have an action plan that you track. Identify anything that may sidetrack your progress and know what you'll do if that happens.

And find regular ways to celebrate the changes!

Use your brain to make this the year you join 9% of people who reach their goals. And imagine how doing this every year will improve your life! Consider the four steps in this chapter *your* magical blowtorch!

WHAT YOU KNOW

- Only goals have the power to help you create something better, because they are clear and require action. Don't confuse them with the other three terms:
    1. *Goal:* a result you can attain but will require intentional action and often cooperation with others to get there
    2. *Wish*: a desire or hope that something could happen (or to want something that cannot or probably will not happen)
    3. *Expectation:* a strong belief that something will happen or be the case in the future
    4. *Resolution:* a firm decision to do or not to do something

- Use this process to set then start achieving your goals:
    1. Step #1: create your communication goal by answering:
        a. What's my point?
        b. Why does it matter?
        c. Then focus this by determining the type of communication you're doing:
        d. Inform
        e. Request
        f. Record
        g. Instruct
        h. Persuade

    2. Step #2: brainstorm your goals, using freewriting (if you're right-brained) and mind mapping (if you're left-brained).
    3. Step #3: pick the three most important goals, because that's the bandwidth for your brain.
    4. Step #4: have a plan and track your progress, preparing for possible breakdowns in advance and celebrating progress along the way.

WHAT TO DO NOW

Immediate Gratification Goal-Setting Worksheet

Use this as a guide to setting goals for short-term and long-term situations. I suggest you start with something smaller—like a meeting, call, or memo—to figure out what works best for you.

1. What is the issue/situation and who are the people involved? (***Stop*** in the Open Mindset Signal™.)

   ____

   ____

   ____

2. Step #1: Create your *communication* goal by answering these questions: (***Explore***.in the Open Mindset Signal™.)

   a. What kind of business communication is this? (circle your answer)
      - Inform
      - Request
      - Record
      - Instruct
      - Persuade

   b. What's my point?

   ____

   ____

c. Why does it matter?

d. Write your communication goal here.

3. Step #2: On the next page (or a blank sheet of paper) use freewriting or mind mapping to brainstorm your goals for five minutes, (You may want to choose one the first time and try the other the next time to see which works best for you.) (***Explore***)

4. Step #3: Review all of the ideas from Step #2.

    a. Write the three most relevant and important action goals here: (***Explore***)

    b. Rewrite your communication goal here, so you have it on the same page for easy reference. (***Go*** in the Open Mindset Signal™.)

    c. Review this goal sheet before you do the communication. (***Go***)

d. Afterward, record your experience: what you learned and how close you came to meeting your communication goal. (***Explore***)

____

____

____

____

e. How was this different from the last time you did something similar *without* setting communication and action goals beforehand? (***Explore***)

____

____

____

____

5. Step #4: Have a plan and track your progress for reaching longer term goals. Prepare yourself and your team for success in these two ways: (***Explore***)

   a. In advance, list the possible breakdowns you'll face and strategies for either preventing or dealing with these.

Potential Breakdown	How I'll Prevent or Deal with This

b. What are your plans for celebrating progress and rewarding the people involved in this (including yourself): (***Explore***)

6. Each day, set goals for one or more business or personal situations and monitor your success rate. (***Go***)

PART 2

"P" IS FOR PEOPLE

Not Just Knowing Who They Are, But How to Connect with Them Based on How Their Brains Work

P = PEOPLE

CHAPTER 4

Stop *Guessing* About Others

We often think we know someone better than we do—or know why we make decisions—and that leads to trouble.

William and I agreed to meet at a Starbucks for a one-hour networking coffee. I was excited! He was president of a market research company. His work sounded interesting, and I wanted to learn more. Plus I was hoping he felt the same, and we could find ways to help each other.

"What do you love about working in market research?" I asked.

William launched into a monologue, sharing what his company did in excruciating detail.

Five minutes in, I realized that William would talk for the next *50* minutes!

He kept his eyes downcast, and pushed papers toward me with marketing data to support his points. Then he pulled out his laptop and started walking me through his website.

This wasn't how I expected things to go. Often networking sessions were evenly divided. He'd talk about his business for 25 minutes, then I'd do the same. Once we knew more about each other, we'd spend the last 10 minutes figuring out specific people to introduce that person to, or other good networking opportunities that made sense.

Not so here.

The voice inside my head went snarky. "He's going to blather on the whole time about what he does. He doesn't even *care* about me and what I do! I'm just an audience for him. How egotistical can you be? When's the soonest I can get the heck out of here?"

I was in reactivity. Acting on that urge would have been a mistake.

MIND THE GAP IN YOUR BRAIN

In Chapter 2, we talked about how our brains are negative, live in the past, and are lazy. I'll reiterate this happens because our conscious mind has limited bandwidth—in a world with limitless stimulation. There's only so much information we can process, requiring our brain to find ways to cope with the overload. So it searches for patterns and takes shortcuts.

That's what was happening as I sat across from William. First, I was looking for patterns. These were similar situations that happened before, or types of people I'd already run into. Rather than spending the time or energy to get to know *William*, I could apply the yardstick of previous experience to make guesses about him—and conserve my brainpower.

If I found William was like others I'd dealt with, then I could do the second thing—find a shortcut. This meant applying the same strategies to interacting with him that had worked with others—such as cutting my losses and getting out of Starbucks ASAP.

You can see the problem here. I'm *filling in the gaps of my knowledge about William with information that has nothing to do with him*—just judgments from my experiences with others. Even worse, *I'm treating my opinions as though they're facts.* My inner voice had labeled William as "egotistical" and dismissive of me based on five minutes with him.

ENTER UNCONSCIOUS BIAS

Unconscious bias is "a learned assumption, belief or stereotype we're not aware of." It prejudices us in favor of—or against—people, situations, or things. Then it's activated without our awareness or intention, and influences our perceptions and actions.

The tough thing about unconscious bias is that we don't know we're doing it. And it's often counter to our conscious beliefs.

This bias happens because our brain is taking a shortcut. When it comes to people or groups, we put them into categories to save time. Then we create social stereotypes to explain these categories: without noticing we're doing that.

We mostly associate bias with matters of race. But it can also be based on age, gender, gender identity, physical abilities, religion, sexual orientation, weight, and pretty much any other characteristic (pattern) you can name.

Here are the most common ones. I've broken them into two groups.

The first one is perception biases about *people*. This happens when we judge or treat others based on inaccurate, overly simplistic stereotypes and assumptions about the person or group to which we think they belong.

1. ***Affinity Bias:*** We prefer someone we have something in common with or believe is like us.

   For example, I have a redheaded friend who interviewed in a department where the manager, and all his people, had blonde hair. She asked him if hair color was a dealbreaker. First he was shocked at the question, then looked around and noticed what she saw!
2. ***Ageism***: We often find this at work: discriminating against people—usually older or younger—because we associate traits with their age group.
3. ***Attribution Bias:*** We tend to believe our achievements come from our personality and efforts. When we don't succeed, it was due to 1) external forces that prevented us from doing our best, or 2) the situation was somehow rigged against us or favored someone else. But we flip this when looking at others. We think of their successes as more due to chance, and their failures stem from their personal shortcomings or behaviors.

   This often happens when we get passed over for a promotion or don't get picked for a new job or plum assignment. It feels more soothing to our egos to blame someone else than admit any failing or misstep from us.
4. ***Authority Bias***: We tend to believe that a leader (someone higher up in the organization, more experienced, or a celebrity) knows more, and we should follow that person's directions.
5. ***Gender Bias***: We favor one gender over others because of the stereotypes we associate with each.
6. ***Beauty Bias***: We treat people better—and have a higher opinion of them—when we think they're attractive. We also can be more distrustful or dismissive of those we deem as not good-looking. (This often leads to the halo and horns effects.)
7. ***Halo Effect***: Once we see a characteristic or action we like, we let that positive glow color every other opinion we have

about that person. Even if we've never seen him/them/her do something—such as make charitable donations to a cause we like—we firmly believe the person has done this.

8. ***Horns Effect:*** After we notice something we *don't* like about a person, we tend to attribute other negative traits or actions to them/her/him. (We're back to me believing that William was egotistical.)
9. ***Idiosyncratic Rater Bias***: We often rate others' performance more on our subjective interpretations (of any assessment criteria) and our own definition of how "success" looks than what people *actually are doing*. When it comes to evaluating employees, research indicates about 60% of a manager's rating reflects the *manager* rather than the *employee*[9].
10. ***Names Bias***: We prefer certain names over others. In the U.S., this most often is Anglo-sounding names. In other countries, these usually are the more familiar names in their culture. (That tracks back to the perceived safety of affinity bias.)
11. ***Racial Bias***: Those who don't look, act, or sound like us can trigger people to apply inaccurate and overly simplistic stereotypes, or show fearful or angry reactions.

The second group of biases involves how we *make decisions and choose to act*:

1. ***Affect Heuristic***: A "heuristic" is a fast and practical shortcut for solving problems or decision-making. You already know you make decisions in your emotional brain. This term covers times when you want to decide something quickly, so you are overly influenced by how you feel right now. The result is you crowd out other factors, such as consequences. (If I'd

9 Buckingham, Marcus, "Most HR Data is Bad Data," February 9, 2015, Harvard Business Review. Viewed at https://hbr,org/2015.02/most-hr-data-is-bad-data on April 18, 2025.

kissed off my meeting with William—because I was angry with what appeared to be his disinterest—that would qualify.)

2. ***Anchor Bias:*** We are overly affected by the first piece of information we have or remember about a subject. Unfortunately, many times it's irrelevant: such as remembering how much we paid for something 10 years ago (a gallon of gas is a good example). This makes the current cost seem extraordinarily high. That means we can end up making a poor choice or feeling taken advantage of.
3. ***Confirmation Bias:*** Once we have an idea or opinion, we look for information to support it. And when we encounter anything that disagrees with or disproves our stance, we give it less weight in our decision-making, or find fault with and discount it. And no amount of factual information will sway us.

   All we have to do here is look at the echo chamber of social media or the places we get our news. We prefer to believe that those who don't agree with us are sloppy, stupid, or self-involved.
4. ***Conformity Bias***: We change our opinions or behaviors to sync with a group that we're in, even when that isn't what we believe. This comes from our ancient urge not to be kicked out of the tribe for being too different.
5. ***Contrast Effect***: How we perceive or understand something is influenced by its context—what we experience before or after it—or something that we immediately compare it to. This can drastically change our opinion—for better or worse—of something's value or quality.

   You experience this every time a salesperson presents a high-cost item, then offers a discount to you, which makes it feel more affordable.
6. ***Illusory Correlation***: Sometimes we imagine there's a relationship between two people, behaviors or events, even when

there is no logical connection. This can lead us to believe superstitions, folk tales, and stereotypes. (A friend of mine won't watch a Chicago Bears football game without his "lucky" team logo glass.)

7. ***Overconfidence Bias***: We can believe our skills and abilities are better than they actually are. For example, research indicates 65% of Americans think they have above-average intelligence.[10]
8. ***Recency Bias***: We can give more importance to things that happened more recently, primarily because these are easier to remember.
9. ***Retrospective Bias***: Our recollection and evaluation of past events or outcomes can be distorted, because these are influenced by the information and experiences we encountered *since* then. For example, we may overestimate how well we can predict an event *after* it has happened. This may skew our understanding of cause and effect and give us an inflated opinion of our foresight.
10. ***Status Quo Bias***: This occurs when we find safety in continuing to do what we've done before, avoiding the risks involved with a new approach.

YES, YOU'RE BIASED. WHAT NOW?

To keep you safe, your brain wants you to hang around with people who look, think, and act like you. And to believe the best of them, and to be suspicious of those who are different. To believe you've had to work hard to get ahead, and others who already arrived got

---

10 Heck, P. R., Simons, D. J., & Chabris, C. F. (2018). 65% of Americans believe they are above average in intelligence: Results of two nationally representative surveys. Viewed at https://journals.plos.org/plosone/article?id=10.1371/journal.pone.0200103 on April 18, 2025.

there unfairly. To believe the best ideas are the older ones—or even that the past is better than the present.

You do these things automatically. It doesn't mean you're a bad person. It *does* mean when you act on these, that you're an unaware one.

Now that you know you default to these biases, do three things to improve your awareness.

First, when you think you may be dealing with your own unconscious bias, ***answer three questions***:

1. ***How have I reacted to this (person, thing, situation, or group) before?*** Create a mental or written list of how this has shown up for you. (In the Open Mindset Signal™, this is *Stop*.)
2. ***Why did I do that?*** Sift through your own thoughts, feelings and behaviors. Then notice the patterns in each. (*Explore)*
3. ***What's a better way to handle that now?*** We've all screwed up and acted on cruise control, were winging it, or were looking for a way to justify what we've done. You don't ask this question to shame yourself. Your goal is to know you have other tools at your disposal, which you can explore the next time you find yourself here. (*Go*)

Those questions help you ensure these biases are no longer unconscious. Now you're not merely reacting and are ready to create better outcomes.

Second, invite others to challenge you. Unconscious biases are deeply ingrained, so you're unlikely to notice all of them all the time. Let people you trust know you're working on this. Ask for their help.

You may try something like, "If you ever see me dismissing an idea from you or someone else because it's different from mine, please tell me."

Then the important work begins. You'll likely be startled at first when someone mentions you seemed awfully dismissive about a different approach and sure yours was the best way. Your predilection will be to defend yourself—especially if the comment is made in front of others. It takes that extra moment to remember this isn't a criticism but an invitation to be a better version of yourself.

Before replying, take a deep breath and consider what was said.

When you respond, be honest and appreciative. These points may help (you'll find the right words to suit you):

1. "I didn't realize that's how I was coming off."
2. "You're right: it looks like I wasn't open to that new idea."
3. "I promise to give this more thought and get back to [whom]."
4. "Thanks for taking the risk of pointing this out to me. I appreciate it and will pay more attention to how I respond to ideas that differ from mine."

Then keep your word. If appropriate, let the person who offered you the feedback know what happened and how this is changing your approach.

Third, speak up. You're getting a gift from the person who lets you know when unconscious bias appears to be affecting *your* actions. You can be that for others—if they're open to it. This can start by you asking for their help because you're working on this. Then you may offer to do the same for them.

We spend enough time in meetings that it's easy to identify those who thoughtlessly put down others or their ideas. What that ultimately does is silence innovation, drive away talented people, and make those who stay less likely to do anything but agree.

People notice you in those sessions. Make it clear that everyone has the right to share an idea so it may be evaluated on its worth. That denigrating others isn't acceptable—and those who do will be asked to stop. And that advancement here is based on merit, so we all get to be inspired by and celebrate those who move ahead. Then you'll be chipping away at unconscious bias—and the limits inherent in it—in yourself and your organization.

What happened in my meeting with William—because he didn't agree with my way to have a networking coffee? Check out the next chapter!

WHAT YOU KNOW

- Your brain searches for patterns and shortcuts for two reasons:
    1. Preserve energy and send it to places that need it.
    2. Your brain doesn't have the bandwidth to process all the stimulation coming at you
- The result is unconscious bias: a prejudice we aren't aware of that favors or discriminates against people, situations, or things, then influences our thoughts and actions.
    1. *People perception biases*:
        a. We judge or treat others based on inaccurate, overly simplistic stereotypes and assumptions about the person or group to which we think they belong
        b. Here are the most common ones: affinity bias, ageism, attribution, authority, beauty, gender, halo effect, horns effect, and idiosyncratic rater
    2. *Decision-making biases*:
        a. We use short-cuts to spend less time thinking before making a choice and acting
        b. Here are the most common ones: affect heuristic, confirmation, conformity, contrast effect, illusory correlation, overconfidence, regency, and status quo
- Use three techniques to be aware of your biases:
    1. Answer three questions on your thoughts and behavior:
        a. How have I reacted to this before?
        b. Why did I do that?
        c. Do I see a better way?
    2. Invite others to tell you when they believe you show unconscious bias
    3. Speak up when you see others showing unconscious bias

WHAT TO DO NOW

Understand the Impact of Unconscious Bias

1. Review the types of people perception biases. Pick one you suspect you might have used. Write it here: (***Stop*** in the Open Mindset Signal™.)

____

____

2. Describe the situation where you believe you applied this to a person or group: (***Explore*** in the Open Mindset Signal™.)

____

____

3. What happened after you said or did something you believe was affected by this bias? (***Explore***)

____

____

4. What do you *wish* had happened instead? (***Explore***)

____

____

Imagine a Better Result Without Unconscious Bias

1. Review the types of decision-making biases. Pick one you want to work on and write it here: (***Stop***)

   ____

   ____

2. Describe the situation where you believe this may happen: (***Explore***)

   ____

   ____

3. How would you answer these questions in that moment: (***Explore***)

   a. How have I reacted to this (person, thing, situation, or group) before?

      ____

      ____

   b. Why did I do that?

      ____

      ____

c. What's a better way to handle that now? (*Go* in the Open Mindset Signal™.)

____

____

Know Which Unconscious Biases Will Likely Affect You

1. Check the ones you'll probably default to: (***Stop***)

___ Affinity ___ Ageism ___ Attribution

___ Authority ___ Beauty ___ Gender

___ Halo effect ___ Horns effect ___ Idiosyncratic rater

___ Names ___ Racial ___ Affect heuristic

___ Anchor ___ Confirmation ___ Conformity

___ Contrast effect ___ Illusory correlation

___ Overconfidence ___ Recency ____ Retrospective

___ Status quo

2. Of these, write which one you want to focus on stopping first, and why: (***Explore***)

____

____

Asking for Help

1. Who are the people you trust to ask for help—and will listen to—as part of reducing the effects of your unconscious bias: at home, work, and other situations? (***Explore***)

____

____

2. How—and when—will you ask them to help? (***Go***)

____

____

3. Who are the people *you* need to speak with about *their* unconscious bias when you see it, and what will you say to them? (***Go***)

____

____

P = PEOPLE

CHAPTER 5

Start *Understanding* Others

It's easy to make others "wrong" when they don't act the way we want them to. This changes when we see what they value, what they fear, and how they like to be treated.

The last chapter started with my having a networking coffee with William, the head of a market research firm. He had turned the conversation into a monologue about how he started the company and what it does.

My unconscious bias was 1) turning him into a self-involved gasbag (horns effect) because 2) he wasn't acting according to my belief that we should get equal time to speak about what we did (confirmation bias). As a result, I was looking to get away from him as soon as possible.

Here's what stopped me.

I took a deep breath and started paying closer attention to William. He was fascinated by the different ways there were to collect data—on subjects as broad as potential international markets for a new product, to why employee turnover was so high at an organization. Each issue required him to design a unique way to uncover information. And that was just the beginning! It was making sense of what he collected, then presenting this to the client—often with recommendations on what to do next—that lit up William.

That's when I realized he was a man who lived for details and digging into how things worked. And he was treating me as though I thought the same way. So William's descriptions—which were like taking the local versus the express train—were an effort to build rapport with *me*! (As you already noticed, he was off target there.)

That led me to ask myself two questions.

First, *does William know people who should know me?* This is a networking meeting, after all, and an important reason for me to be here. I believed the answer was yes.

Second, *am I willing to pay the price of sitting here and listening carefully to build rapport with William, so he'll feel comfortable introducing me to those people?* I considered this for a moment (the idea of running away was still appealing). Then decided I was willing to stay.

Here's the big surprise.

After making that choice, I stopped being judgmental about William and making him "wrong" for not following the rules in *my* head. I got more relaxed and interested in what he was saying—because I knew why I was there. (If I'd done the goal work in Chapter 3 before this meeting, I would have saved myself a lot of angst and snarkiness.)

At five minutes before the top of the hour, William turned to me and asked, "So, what do *you* do?" I'm a get-crap-done kind of person, so I could answer that in the allotted time.

Then something magical happened. William introduced me to a man who became a great client of mine for years, and who referred me to other good people. None of this would have happened if I'd acted on my instincts (driven by unconscious bias) and bailed.

ONE OF OUR BIGGEST MISTAKES WITH PEOPLE

This is one I made with William. I believed my approach of "dividing networking time equally" was the best one. As such, I thought William should agree and act accordingly.

We default to treating everyone as though they're just like us. And when they show us they aren't, we think it's their *issue.* After that, we often seek to show them the error of their ways. We can use "constructive criticism" and other approaches, which push them away and usually make any problem bigger.

Are you ready to get off that merry-go-round of dissatisfaction? Here's what's worked for me—and lots of others I've worked with.

THE BLESSING OF A FOUR QUADRANT PERSONALITY PROFILE

There are plenty of good, thoughtful systems out there to help you know more about people's personalities—yours and others. Find one that works and stick with it. My only suggestion is that it be easy to apply to other people—especially those you don't yet know well.

I love DISC® for the detailed insights it can offer about how *I* show up in the world. It's a four-quadrant approach, standing for Dominance, Influence, Steadiness, and Conscientiousness. But I have two issues with this approach. First, the report on each personality style can run nearly 100 pages, which can be a lot to digest. Second, I have a hard time sitting across from others in a meeting and quickly figuring out who *they* are. (Some of this may be *my* issue, but people I trust have told me they have the same problem.)

This is why I prefer four quadrant methods that are simpler. Of course they are more general. If you have five or more personality types to determine who someone is (the Enneagram has nine) then you won't have time to actually pay attention to her/them/him! (You already know the limits on your conscious brain processing abilities.)

What you're trying to do is get a good initial sense of what someone values, is afraid of, and how they like to be communicated with. There are three benefits to this:

1. ***It gives you a head-start in getting to know that person.*** (You'll fill in the gaps with real information about people as you get to understand them better.)
2. ***It reduces your judgments—and annoyance—about their behavior.*** (My line about this is "you can't punish people for being who they are"— what I was about to do with William.)
3. ***It offers a way to build faster connections***, because you know how they like to receive information and be treated. (This reduces the time you might waste—and repair work you need to do—when you've *not* communicated in the way they prefer.)

Four-quadrant systems are based on a matrix of active versus passive, and thinking versus feeling. In creating the MIND Reader Method™, I used the same approach. Here's how I placed the four personality types:

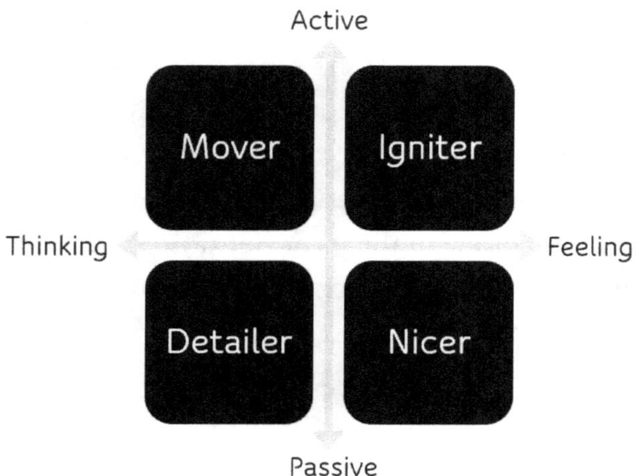

This is a quick summary of what you're seeing:

- ***Movers*** are active thinkers. They want to be in charge and value doing, achieving, action, and leading. They are concerned about outcomes, the big picture, and preventing others from taking advantage of them. They don't care about extreme detail, being popular, and their or others' emotions.
- ***Igniters*** are active feelers. They love to motivate people and value change, appreciation, recognition, activity, and excitement. They are concerned about losing the approval of others and being ignored. They don't focus on outcomes, accuracy, or following others.
- ***Nicers*** are passive feelers. They are peacemakers who value people, feelings, listening, relationships, and having everyone get along. They are concerned about losing affection or being left out. They aren't interested in accuracy, control, or excitement.
- ***Detailers*** are passive thinkers. They value accuracy, precision, security, being correct, and having the facts. They are concerned about criticism of their work, being wrong, and making mistakes. They wish to have respect and are hurt when

they don't get it. They have little interest in time, popularity, or being liked.

We have the most difficulty with those who are kitty-corner to us in this matrix:

- Movers like to get things done, so can be frustrated by Nicers, who are more interested in having everyone get along.
- Nicers see Movers as brusque, controlling, and uninterested in having good relationships.
- Igniters want to lead change and can lose patience with Detailers' desire to dot "i"s and cross "t"s.
- Detailers experience Igniters as people who like the spotlight and aren't thoughtful about how things should be done.

Let's take a closer look at each style. You are a mixture of all four, but pay attention to the one that seems most like you.

MOVERS MAKE THINGS HAPPEN

Movers tend to be leaders. They're doers, very goal-oriented, and tend to take charge. ***Getting things done*** is their greatest strength. They like to organize and spearhead, and they do it well.

Movers take an intellectual approach when dealing with people and usually respond assertively to problems and situations.

MOVERS AT A GLANCE

Characteristics	Care About
• Thinking • Independent • Assertive • Purposeful • Direct to the point/speak their minds • Are wary if others hesitate • Direct people without hesitation/take charge • Cool and in control • Abrupt or short • Workaholic	• Doing • Achieving goals • Action • Leading • Getting results
Not as Concerned About	**Need**
• Feelings • Analysis • Approval • Others • Being a team player	• To feel things are well-run • Challenge • To win • To see a purpose • Reasons without too much detail
Are Afraid of	
• Losing control • Being taken advantage of	

Movers want to get right into action. They need just enough information to make a decision. They can get impatient with too much data (because they already decided what to do and don't need more) and with others who are taking too long to decide. They also need to feel they are in control of any situation. Although they can come off as cool and confrontational, Movers' ability to strive for the best can make them rewarding people to work with.

***If you** are **a Mover**,* you may need to temper your impatience when people hesitate, have trouble making decisions, or give you too much information. Learning how to do "small talk" to show your interest in others also will serve you well.

***If you're** not **a Mover**,* know they can appear unfriendly. They may also provide an authority against which others would like to rebel. Movers expect people to be on time, accurate, and effective. They expect to tell you something once, and then you go do it. When this doesn't happen, Movers let you know directly and immediately.

If you're presenting information or ideas to a Mover, executive summaries are best. Give the key points and be prepared with the details in your head to answer their questions. They won't read long documents and will resent you for foisting these on them. When you can tie what you're proposing to a goal you know they want to reach, and show how this will get them there faster, you'll gain their attention.

As leaders, you may find you either love them or hate them, depending on how well you work with strong personalities.

IGNITERS MOTIVATE US

Igniters are ***creative and full of ideas.*** They can be enthusiastic and inspiring: they are natural in sales and service-oriented work. However, sometimes they can lose interest in follow-through and don't take deadlines and rules seriously. Enthusiasm is the Igniter's greatest strength. They inspire and lead by believing deeply in what they say and do.

Igniters value feelings when dealing with people, and respond assertively when handling problems.

IGNITERS AT A GLANCE

Characteristics	Care About
• Talkative • Creative • Energetic • Outgoing • High risk-takers • Charming/the life of the party • Attention-getters • Smile • Crack jokes • Inspirational • Don't pay attention to time • Feeling and assertive • Take time to get to the point	• Appreciation • Change • Activity • Excitement
Not as Concerned About	**Need**
• Deadlines • Rules • Goals	• Compliments, recognition • Approval • Lots of activity
Are Afraid of	
• Others not admiring and appreciating them • Others not following them	

Igniters make others feel positive, excited and inspired. They are always ready to try something new.

If you are ***an Igniter***, you may need to find ways to keep yourself on track. Depending on whom you're with, you may be called on to temper your creativity, enthusiasm, and talkative nature by learning to listen more.

If you're not ***an Igniter***, know they don't care about time and won't understand if you can't accommodate them when they're late. They may feel hurt, and can get angry, when they aren't getting attention and approval from others. They usually let you know if they don't like something you've done.

Your ideas will be welcomed when you enthusiastically show Igniters how this will make them look even better to key audiences (such as clients, board members, senior leaders, etc.). Combine this with a willingness to have others handle the details and keep things moving, and you'll capture their attention.

Igniters encourage you to bring your full creativity. They give you the most opportunity to express yourself. You'll need to make sure your Igniter friends and colleagues feel important and appreciated.

Igniters flow with ideas—but sometimes fall short on delivery.

NICERS CARE ABOUT EVERYONE

Nicers get along with everyone and try to make sure each person is happy. They tend to ***have the most "heart."*** At the same time, they are more likely to be late getting a job done, because they have less interest in the amount of time a task is taking than in people and their feelings.

When dealing with others, Nicers orient themselves to feelings and tend to respond passively when it comes to problems.

NICERS AT A GLANCE

Characteristics	Care About
• Open • Patient • Passive • Willing to listen • Smile • Seldom criticize • Chat easily • Remember your last conversation • Good listeners • Not risk-takers • Enthusiastic • Can silently hold a grudge	• People • Feelings • Relationships
Not as Concerned About	**Need**
• Time • Tasks • Productivity	• To be accepted • To be liked • To get along • Cooperation • To talk about feelings and have their feelings recognized or considered • Measured (not fast) movement
Are Afraid of	
• Being left out • Conflict • People not getting along	

Nicers make you feel the best about yourself and your work. They are friendly and personable, unless they are painfully shy. They make sure that you feel special when they interact with you. You may find you have the warmest feelings toward the Nicers in your life.

Nicers' friendly and welcoming nature may foster *team spirit*, but not always *teamwork*. The latter requires a focus on completing tasks. This tends not to be their main concern.

Nicers aren't likely to take risks. They don't want to make anyone angry. That's one reason they avoid conflict whenever possible. This can mean Nicers won't tell you directly that they're angry, hurt, sad, or afraid because of something you've done. They're more likely to tell someone else, or treat you with a bit more distance and expect you to pick up on it.

If you are ***a Nicer***, you usually need support to stay on schedule. Since getting the job done on time isn't your strength, ask for help. Pay attention to the times when your fear of conflict prevents you from having conversations that help to clear the air.

If you're not ***a Nicer***, know they can be indecisive. They often have a hard time making up their minds and stating their preferences, which can leave you guessing.

When you want to persuade a Nicer, move slowly and maintain rapport. Consider their desire for acceptance, being liked, and the importance they place on feelings. You need to move them to decisions in a respectful way, without making them feel rushed or pressured. Also explain how your plan will get others involved in working together and be recognized for their efforts.

Nicers are great to be around, as long as deadlines aren't an issue.

DETAILERS GET TO THE BOTTOM OF THINGS

Detailers are factual, precise, and thorough people. They generally don't like change and are less likely to chitchat. ***Organization and accuracy*** are their greatest gifts. They take a structured, logical approach to work and understand the facts of a situation. Detailers are "in their head" when dealing with people, and passive and methodical in responding to problems.

DETAILERS AT A GLANCE

Characteristics	Care About
• Focus • Hesitancy • Neatness • Shyness • Deal in facts • Worry about the time • Focus on concrete details • Listen intently and respond after reflection • Low risk-takers • Slower paced • Conservative • Wordy	• Accuracy • Perfection • Precision • Security
Not as Concerned About	**Need**
• Speed • Feelings • Friends	• Security • Time to think • Facts to rely on • Order • Predictability

Are Afraid of	
• Making mistakes • Being wrong • Not getting respect	

Detailers tend to be quiet. They may work intently, though slowly, through a project or challenge. Detailers can be counted on to follow directions to the letter. They tend to make others feel secure and safe.

Detailers are not socializers. They are less likely to make small talk and can appear cold and stand-offish. Others may feel frustrated that Detailers do not react well to change or don't clearly say what they want. Like Nicers, they don't often take risks.

When they're passionate about something, or when they're presenting a case for their ideas, Detailers will give you infinite detail: more than any other personality style wants or needs. Because they're afraid of making a mistake, Detailers use data to support their position. They can make people wait for their decisions because they can't get enough information to feel comfortable choosing a direction.

If you are ***a Detailer***, you excel where precision counts. Know others don't need as much information as you do so may feel frustrated and overwhelmed by the amount of data you provide. It helps them if you focus on the important points and let them know you can share more if they like.

If you're not ***a Detailer***, you'll better connect with them by focusing on consistency, facts, and methods. They prefer the 10-page report to the executive summary. When they see too little data, they judge those responsible as being sloppy and not doing their homework.

They also love to get into the weeds. It helps to consider all of the questions you're likely to be asked before a meeting and be ready to answer these. That way, you won't have to come back a second (or third) time. Having appendices on PowerPoints at the back of your presentation, or on paper that you may pass to them, reinforces your position as informed and thorough. This makes it easier for them to say "yes."

Don't expect them to be forthcoming. You'll also need to make sure your Detailer friends and colleagues feel secure, which means offering them consistency and sameness.

OPEN UP YOUR EYES AND YOUR WORLD

Now you can see that William is a Detailer and I'm a Mover. That's why he defaulted to sharing minutia, while I only wanted the salient ideas he could cover in 25 minutes. This was the disconnect—compounded by my judgments based on unconscious bias—that threatened to derail opportunities for each of us to be of service to each other.

There are plenty of times we wish people were more like us. Boy are we wrong!

- A world of Movers means everyone would want to lead—and nothing would get done.
- A world of Igniters means everyone wants others to act on their ideas—and no one is interested in how to make this happen.
- A world of Nicers means everyone is concerned that no one be left out—and this focus leaves no time for doing the work.
- A world of Detailers means no decisions will be made—because there's never enough data to remove the risk from any option.

When you're having trouble working or getting along with someone, start here. Know your primary style. Pay attention to how others behave and make an educated guess on their style. Notice what others value and fear. Then you'll spend less time punishing them for not being *you* and more time framing your approach in a way that connects with *them*.

If you want to know more about the MIND Reader Method™, visit www.yourwordsmith.com/MindReader. You may order the tool, take about 10 minutes to do it, and receive a more detailed analysis for yourself and your team.

WHAT YOU KNOW

- It's easy to apply a four-quadrant personality approach to get an initial understanding of a new acquaintance—and even those we know well. These are based on a simple matrix: thinking versus feeling, and active versus passive.
- Here's a quick summary of each style, using the MIND Reader Method™:
  1. ***Movers*** (active thinkers) want to be in charge; aren't as concerned with people, feelings, or details; are afraid of losing control.
  2. ***Igniters*** (active feelers) want to motivate others; aren't as concerned about goals and outcomes; are afraid people won't appreciate them.
  3. ***Nicers*** (passive feelers) want everyone to get along; aren't as concerned about productivity and deadlines; are afraid of being left out.
  4. ***Detailers*** (passive thinkers) want more data to increase their accuracy; aren't as concerned with speed; are afraid of making a mistake.
- When you're struggling to work or connect with someone, know what your primary style is and make an educated guess about the other person's. Know you have the most difficulty with those who are kitty-corner to you in the matrix:
  1. Movers have trouble with Nicers, because these people don't value getting things done.
  2. Igniters have issues with Detailers, because these people love to share too much data with them.
  3. Nicers can struggle with Movers, because these people often are abrupt and don't value feelings.
  4. Detailers have difficulty with Igniters, because these people don't want all the information they wish to provide.

WHAT TO DO NOW

Understanding Yourself, Colleagues, Family and Friends

1. My primary personality style is: (***Stop*** in the Open Mindset Signal™.)

    ____

    ____

    ____

2. Here's how I describe myself: (***Explore*** in the Open Mindset Signal™.)

    a. I value:

    ____

    ____

    ____

    b. I need:

    ____

    ____

    ____

c. I'm afraid of:

____

____

____

3. Write the name of a person (someone at work, a client, a family member or friend) you've had a difficult relationship with: (***Explore***)

____

____

____

4. Describe a situation where the two of you didn't agree or were in conflict: (***Explore***)

____

____

____

5. What do you think that person's primary style is? (***Explore***)

____

____

____

6. In that case, what does this person value, need, and fear? (***Explore***)

7. Now that you know this, how does it change how you view the difficult situation you described with that person? (***Explore***)

8. What are you going to do differently the next time you deal with this person to create a better outcome: (***Go*** in the Open Mindset Signal™.)

   a. What is your goal for this encounter? (If you need a refresh on goals, go to Chapter 3.)

   b. How will you present your ideas in a way that appeals to what she/they/he values?

____

____

c. What things will you *stop* saying or doing because these are ineffective or set off that person?

____

____

____

d. What are the "hot buttons" this person pushes on you?

____

____

____

e. How will you be aware of these and not let them trigger you?

____

____

____

P = PEOPLE

CHAPTER 6

Start *Connecting* with Others

Many times when we struggle to build rapport, it's because the other person has a different thinking style. You can't change yours, but you can adapt to theirs in the moment.

Carlos, the president of a digital marketing agency, told me this story.

He was interviewing candidates for an account representative position the day before. One had him stumped.

On paper, Kris had what Carlos was looking for. The right education. Job experience in creating apps—which was a plus, since many of the agency's clients were in that field. Carlos' head of human resources had contacted two former employers, who described Kris as very conscientious and a hard worker.

"During the whole interview, this man never looked me in the eyes," Carlos explained. "Kris kept staring at the conference table as I spoke. I thought it was because the position didn't appeal to him. Or maybe he was a slacker. I was getting ready to call it quits.

"Then I asked him one more question. 'Can you tell me why you thought you'd be interested in this job?' I didn't expect much of an answer," he added, shrugging his shoulders.

Then Carlos' eyes got wide. "Without looking up, Kris replied, 'I really like what you said about your mission: 'Empowering brands with innovative strategies, our agency is dedicated to delivering exceptional results for clients while nurturing a fulfilling, growth-focused environment for our team. And also the story about how you helped that app start-up stop wasting money on strategies that would never pay off. So you created a website and social media presence that helped double its revenue in nine months. I'd love to be a part of the team that does work like that.'

"It was clear he'd heard everything I said—but I couldn't get a good read on Kris at all," Carlos explained. "Should I hire this guy?"

You can see that Carlos was affected by some unconscious biases about Kris. The information he was getting from the interview was confusing, and his brain was jumping to conclusions trying to make sense of this. (Go to Chapter 4 if you need a refresher.)

Would *you* hire Kris? Here's some information that will help when you're confused by people you don't understand.

READ THEIR BODIES TO READ THEIR MINDS

The VAK model (visual, auditory, kinesthetic) created by educator Neil Fleming, outlines three primary ways that people learn—based on how their brains process information. The good news is you can figure out how people think by watching their body language.

The Looker

This is the most prevalent thinking style: about 75% of people are Lookers. That means they process information—think—visually, mainly in pictures and images. You can identify them by seeing these signs:

1. They have good posture, and hold stress in their shoulders, which means these can be raised and tight.
2. They often have thin lips. (This is a chicken and egg thing. We can't say being a Looker causes thin lips—or vice versa—just that there's a correlation.)
3. They frequently have wrinkles on their foreheads. This happens because people generally look up, raise their eyebrows, furrow their brows and breathe faster when they remember something they have *seen*. Lookers do this often, so their wrinkles are more pronounced.
4. They look in your eyes while speaking and listening.
5. They choose clothes and decorate their offices and homes for visual impact.

If you want to build rapport with Lookers, do two things:

1. ***Speak in images*** whenever possible, since this is how they like to get information. These are the words they use when they talk to themselves, so you're literally speaking their language:
   "I see what you mean."
   "What's your view on this?"
   "Here's what his comments reveal to me."
   "Show me."
   "Take a look at this."
2. ***Look in their eyes*** when listening or speaking. These people believe if you aren't looking at their faces, you aren't paying

attention to them. Eye contact lets them know they are important to you, that you are interested in them, and you're not trying to hide something.

If you're *not* a Looker, don't be unnerved by how much these people look you in the eyes. They're not trying to be confrontational. This is just how they like to get information.

The Listener

About 20% of people are Listeners. These people think mainly in sounds: words and noises. They share these characteristics:

1. Their shoulders usually are slightly rounded.
2. They frequently hold their heads slightly down and to the side. This happens because people look to their left, tilt their heads a bit, and breathe evenly when they remember something they have *heard*. In addition, it naturally points one of their ears in your direction so they can hear you better.
3. They often put a hand up and cradle one side of their face in it while sitting. This is called "telephone posture."
4. Their lips may open or move when they are thinking through something. They also may mumble or speak out loud. This is because they are literally talking to themselves when processing information.
5. They most often look away from others, or close their eyes when speaking or listening.
6. They frequently "drum" with their fingers, click their pens or bang them on the desk or table, and have music on in the background.

Keep these things in mind when communicating with a listener:

1. ***Emphasize sounds*** in your descriptions:
   "I want to hear what you think."
   "That sounds good to me."
   "What does that tell you?"
   "Let's talk about that."
   "I'd like to speak with you."
2. ***Don't give them too much eye contact***: this makes them feel uncomfortable. Look away then back to them when you speak and when you listen.

If you are *not* a Listener, don't feel ignored when you aren't receiving much eye contact. These people still are paying attention to what you are saying—unless they're wearing ear buds!

The Toucher

This group makes up about 5% of the population. They process information through emotions and physical activity. In addition to being more likely to touch people than the other two groups, here's how you can identify them:

1. They tend to lean toward you in a conversation.
2. They frequently look down to their right, round their shoulders and breathe deeply—because this is what people do when remembering something they have *felt*.
3. They generally have full lips and deep voices.
4. Their movements are loose and relaxed.
5. They choose their clothes and design their surroundings based on comfort rather than style.

When talking with a Toucher, use these techniques:

1. ***Emphasize feelings or tactile words*** in your conversation.
   "How do you feel about that?"
   "Let's get in touch."
   "I'm having trouble grasping this."
   "I'm going to contact him."
   "How would you like me to get hold of you?"
2. ***Feel free to touch them*** on the shoulder, arm, or hand when you want to emphasize a point.

If you are *not* a Toucher, don't feel your space is being invaded when they lean in or touch you. This isn't meant to be aggressive. Touchers want to build rapport by decreasing the physical space between themselves and others.

It's true: you may not feel comfortable when a stranger is barreling toward you, wanting to envelope you in a bear hug. The last thing you need to do is stiffen in their grip. Instead, put a hand out to shake theirs. What they're looking for is physical contact. Give them a signal of what kind is OK with you.

What's Your *Style of Thinking?*

That's probably what you're asking now. Of course your brain is flexible, so you can think in all three ways. But just as you have a dominant hand, you have a dominant way of thinking. Here's how to figure out what that is. Read these directions, then give it a go:

1. Close your eyes.
2. Take a deep breath, then remember an important event in your life. Stay with this for a minute.
3. Then pay attention to *how* you're remembering it:
   a. Do you "see" it—in colors, shapes, and pictures—like a movie?

b. Do you describe it in words, or remember what people said?
c. Do you recall how you felt—or how different objects felt in your hands, or something smelled or tasted?

These are the important clues that tell you how *you* think.

Then double-check your answer. Look through what you've written: emails, texts, etc. If you're a Looker, you'll see you use visual words more often. Listeners will use more auditory language, and Touchers will default to feeling and tactile words.

The good news is that you know who you are. The bad news is that you'll automatically treat everyone as though they have the *same* style as you.

That's what was happening with Carlos. He was a Looker. Kris, on the other hand, was a Listener. This explains why he wasn't giving Carlos lots of eye contact. And why Carlos experienced this as disrespect, so was judging Kris as a slacker or uninterested in the position—as a Looker trying to make sense of the experience.

Your Brain Is Here to Help

It's true: giving Lookers more eye contact, giving Listeners less, and reaching for the hand of a Toucher in conversation helps to create rapport. Fortunately, your subconscious mind is also on the case.

We all have something called mirror neurons. They were discovered in studies of monkeys in the 1990s. The upshot is that when the monkeys observed a student eating an ice cream cone, the same neurons fired in the monkeys' brains as if *they* were also eating something!

Mirror neurons are particularly focused on reading facial expressions. Some researchers even postulate that the mirror neurons in those with autism or schizophrenia don't function well, which is why these people have trouble associating meaning with what they see on people's faces. Other experts believe that mirror neurons not only mimic movement and facial expressions but *understand* what they mean.

Here's the important idea for us as persuasive communicators. When we're sitting across from someone, and we see her cradle her chin in her right hand, our brain reacts as though we're doing the same thing. And a lot of times, that's just what *we'll* do.

In a way, our brains are suggesting our bodies copy the behavior of the person we're watching. In the jungle days, this probably was a great survival technique—helping you fit in with the crowd. Now that you know this, you'll notice that you're folding your hands on a conference table the way the person you're in conversation with is doing—or vice versa.

Actively mirroring the physical actions of the person you want to connect with *does* help build rapport. When that person leans in—and you lean in, too—their/his/her unconscious mind registers this as simpatico. You help others feel more comfortable physically, and their brains pick this up as agreeing with them. And you don't even have to think about it. Your brain is automatically helping you to be more persuasive!

Build on this by being aware of the body language of the people you want to reach and mirroring it. Then watch how much faster they are at ease with you.

Quick Note on Verbal Versus Nonverbal Communication

For years, the following numbers have been floating around. That body language accounts for 55% of communication, followed by 38% for voice tone and quality, and 7% from words. Don't believe it!

This was extracted from a study by Albert Mehrabian, Professor Emeritus of Psychology at the University of California. Mehrabian designed his research for a specific application and agrees the figures just mentioned can't be universally applied.

If that's the case, what *is* true?

I appreciate the approach taken by Dr. Jeff Thompson, a research psychologist at Columbia University. He calls this the "3 Cs of Nonverbal Communication."[11]

- ***Context*** includes the environment where the communication is happening, the history between the people involved, plus "other factors, such as each person's role (for example, an interaction between a boss and employee)."
- ***Clusters*** means looking at *all* the types of gestures a person is using, rather than considering only one when trying to determine someone's state of mind or emotion. As Thompson puts it, "crossing your arms at your chest can be a sign of being resistant and close-minded. However, if the person's shoulders are raised and their teeth are chattering, they might just be cold."
- ***Congruence*** involves noticing if the body language, words, and tone of voice match. Let's say someone is glaring at you. You ask, "How are you feeling?" and he/they/she spits out, "Fine." You can sense the disconnect.

Of all these, I think congruence is the most telling. Always believe the body language (in this case, the glare) before the words being said. We know others can lie to us, or be coached on what to say. Most people are unaware of their body language. That means they're less likely to modify it and fool us in the moment.

---

[11] Thompson, Jeff. "Is Nonverbal Communication a Numbers Game?" *Psychology Today,* September 30, 2011. Viewed at https://www.psychologytoday.com/us/blog/beyond-words/201109/is-nonverbal-communication-a-numbers-game on April 18, 2025.

MINDING LOOKERS, LISTENERS AND TOUCHERS

I'm often asked if there's a direct correlation between how people think (Lookers, Listeners. and Touchers) and their personality style (Movers, Igniters, Nicers, and Detailers). As you may have guessed, Carlos was a Mover and Kris was a Detailer.

Statistically speaking, there are three-times as many Lookers as Listeners and Touchers combined. It makes sense that you'll find them in all of the MIND groups. Beyond that, here's what my experience indicates.

Because of their interest in appearance, Lookers can be more common in the active groups: Movers and Igniters. They like being seen and heard, and want others to follow them. So how they present themselves gets others' attention.

Listeners tend to gravitate toward being Detailers and hold more research and technical positions (for which eye contact and social skills are not emphasized). They also can be Nicers—particularly those who are shy.

But there are no direct correlations here. I'm a Listener and a Mover, which shows you need to treat people as individuals.

USE THIS AS ANOTHER SOURCE OF INFORMATION

Your goal is to be more observant of the people you want to persuade. You can't do that without first connecting with them. The more you understand about who they are and how they like to give and receive information, the better you can become at reaching them. And also about making practical decisions.

Now Carlos understood that he and Kris had different personality and thinking styles. He shouldn't dismiss Kris just because they weren't the same.

"I'm serious," Carlos said. "Do you think I should hire him?"

"Let's look at what you know," I replied. "How much client interaction would Kris have?"

"A lot. He'd be the primary contact person for a number of accounts," Carlos said.

"Who would he be working with the most: technical people, communications and marketing people, or senior leaders?"

"Mostly the last two groups."

"Since 75% of people are Lookers, this likely applies to your clients. Do you think they'd have trouble if Kris isn't giving them eye contact?"

"I hadn't thought about that," Carlos answered. "It could be an issue."

"If so, do you think Kris could be teachable? As a Listener, I learned to look at people more often. If he has all the other skills and talents you need, would it be worth investing in building his abilities in this area?"

Carlos smiled. "You've given me a few things to think about and check out. And I'm probably going to make better hiring decisions when I pay attention to this stuff."

It was my turn to smile.

WHAT YOU KNOW

- ***Lookers*** (75% of people) think in images and pictures. Connect with them by giving them lots of eye contact and using "visual" words.

- ***Listeners*** (20%) think in words and sounds. Connect with them by *not* giving them too much eye contact and using "sound" words.

- ***Touchers*** (5%) think in feelings and kinesthetically. Connect with them by leaning in, feeling comfortable with occasional physical contact, and using "feeling" and "tactile" words.

- Mirror neurons in your brain unconsciously encourage you to use the same type of body language as the people you're with. Become aware of the physical behavior and gestures of others and mirror this (in a way that feels natural for you) as another way to build rapport.

- There are no reliable statistics on how much influence verbal versus nonverbal communications have on people. Jeff Thompson's 3 Cs of Nonverbal Communication can be useful:
  1. Pay attention to the ***context***: the setting, the history of the people involved, and other key factors (such as roles in an organization).
  2. When it comes to gestures, notice the ***clusters*** or patterns of these, rather than reaching a conclusion based on a single one.
  3. When words and body language don't match, there is no ***congruence***. Believe the body language—if the lips are smiling and the eyes are not, trust the eyes.

WHAT TO DO NOW

Confirm How Your Brain Works Exercise

1. If you haven't already done the "close your eyes" exercise in this chapter, do it now. Are you a Looker, Listener or Toucher? (***Explore*** in the Open Mindset Signal™.)

 ___

 ___

2. Corroborate your answer. Review at least five emails, texts, reports, etc., you've written with more than five sentences. Record the visual, auditory and feeling/tactile words you used. (***Explore***)

 Visual Words: ___

 ___

 Auditory Words: ___

 ___

 Feeling/Tactile Words: ___

 ___

3. What did you learn? (*Explore*)

____

____

Analyze Your Coworkers or Family Members Exercise

1. Pick four people who are important in your personal and/or professional life.

   ____

2. Determine how they think: Looker, Listener or Toucher. (*Explore*)

   a. ____

   b. ____

   c. ____

   d. ____

3. Choose one of them. Now that you know how he/she/they thinks, how will you change your approach to create better rapport? (*Go* in the Open Mindset Signal™.)

____

____

____

____

Analyze a Person You Haven't Met Exercise

1. Pick someone you've never met in person (they still qualify if you've only seen them in virtual meetings). (*Explore*)

____

____

____

____

2. Review emails or other written correspondence you've received from that person. What type of language are they using, and what style do you guess they are? (*Explore*)

____

____

____

____

3. Check your work. The next time you're in a virtual meeting or on the phone, notice if they're speaking with more visual, auditory, or feeling/tactile words. (***Go***)

____

____

____

____

Now you know you don't even have to be in someone's presence to figure out how her/his/their brains work!

PART 3

"S" IS FOR SHOWCASE

Clearly Present "What's in It for Them" in the Language They Prefer

S = SHOWCASE

CHAPTER 7

Know How to Reach Out

You have achievable goals and a good sense of the people you want to persuade. Know the steps their brains go through to "get" your ideas and how to start that process.

The Chicago Math and Science Academy was hosting an evening program in its high school cafeteria for the senior class and recent graduates. The goal was to have students write their first résumé.

The principal asked me to give a 15-minute keynote to kick things off. The title was "The Power of Résumé." That made *me* want to yawn!

I imagined what the students would be thinking as I stood before them. "They made us turn off our phones to listen to some boring old lady talk about résumés. I'd rather be *anywhere* else!"

How was I going to get them off to a good start, so they'd be motivated to tackle their task that night?

THE PERSUASION CYCLE: GETTING BRAINS TO "YES"

This was the answer. The Persuasion Cycle is one of the most powerful communication ideas I've come across. Mark Goulston[12] developed it, based on the work of Carlo DiClemente and James Prochaska, authors of *Transtheoretical Model of Change*, and by William Miller and Stephen Rollnick, who co-wrote *Motivational Interviewing*.

These are the steps our brains go through to agree to do anything.

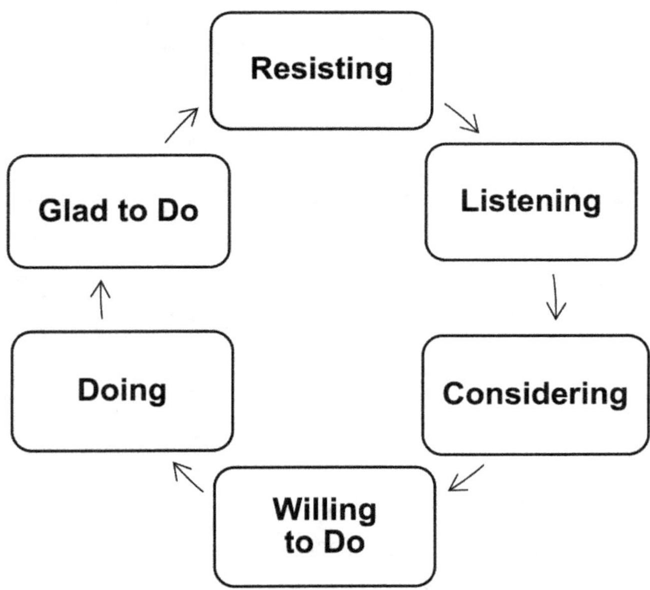

12 Goulston, op. cit., pages 8–10.

Paying Attention to Buy-In

Let's focus on the front end of the cycle: 1) Resisting, 2) Listening, and 3) Considering. There are two reasons for this.

First, these are the steps where we create buy-in from the people we're trying to persuade. If we don't accomplish this, we won't have a shot at the rest of the process to get our ideas accepted.

Second, it's the hardest part of the process. If you're reading this, you're probably passionate about what you and your organization do, or you want to make a difference at home or in the office. This means that, given the opportunity to share your passion, you can be pretty compelling—and you do a good job of handling Willing to Do, Doing, and Glad to Do. Let's work on what to do to get you that opportunity.

Resisting

Everybody begins here. Even people who *want* to agree with you will resist you. The good news is that this has nothing to do with *you*—it's how our brains are wired.

Remember the amygdala? It's still in everyone's brain, looking for risks. Any new ideas need to be evaluated: even the stuff people will love. Until others can be sure what you're proposing isn't harmful—or inconvenient or unnecessary—they will stay stuck in Resisting.

We break through that by getting their attention.

At the Chicago Math and Science Academy, this started with me wandering around the cafeteria in advance. I'd walk up to one student, or a group, and say, "I'm one of the people who is here to help. My name is Lynne. Could you help *me* out first? I'd love to hear what you want to get from tonight so I can make sure that happens."

There were the shy, giggly girls who looked at each other rather than me. They didn't know what to say—and didn't want to give the wrong answer. I encouraged them by asking more questions. "If you could have *any* job, what would you like to do?"

There were the solitary, serious-looking boys. "I want to design video games." "I don't know. But my teacher told me whatever it is, I need a résumé."

After chatting with the boys and girls a bit, I asked their names and thanked them for talking with me. This took me through the first two steps in moving them from Resisting to Listening.

Use the Seven Second Rule. Do you have trouble remembering people's names? Welcome to being human.

Earlier we talked about your conscious mind processing 10–50 bits of information per second. When you meet a new person, for the first seven seconds your brain is overloaded with way more than that. And this is usually when people introduce themselves. Your conscious mind can't process it all, and it throws out their name. Plus, names have no inherent meaning in our brains. Unless we can make an immediate association with a name ("My brother also is a Mark.") our brain dumps it.

On top of that, in western cultures our first name is the most important word in the language to us. That means our brains are conspiring against us to remember the word that creates a connection with the other person!

Change that by using my *Seven Second Rule*. Never ask for a name or introduce yourself in the first seven seconds of meeting a new person: you don't have the bandwidth to remember it. But you can't stand there silently for seven seconds without being creepy! Instead, do one of these two things:

1. Ask a question, such as, "What do you think of the conference so far?" and let them answer.
2. Make a statement, for example, "I didn't expect the weather would be so hot today!" and let them respond.

By the time they do, seven seconds have gone by. You're now able to focus on their face and ask their name. They'll likely give you their first and last names, but (in western cultures) you only need to remember their first. Say it out loud a few times, looking them in the eyes (even if you're a Listener), which will move it into your long-term memory.

Waiting until the students and I had talked a while before asking for their names helped me to remember what they said.

Listen First. Most of us wander through life feeling chronically unseen and unheard. A great way to move people from Resisting to Listening is by listening yourself—and giving them *all* of your attention.

There are two types of listening.

Listening to respond is the most common. You pay attention to what people say, so you'll know what to say when they stop talking. This gets you *data,* but it won't bring *connection*—or move people out of resisting.

Listening for understanding and empathy is more valuable. You pay attention not just to information, but body language, tone of voice, and emotions. This gives you a better sense of the whole person.

Research shows that listening for understanding and empathy engages two parts of the speaker's brain. First, their reward centers: as if they're getting money or doing something they like. Second, the part of the brain involved in evaluating positive emotions: which they now associate with you.

There are three more bonuses:

1. *Benefiting from the Rule of Reciprocity*—When you listen well, you build good will. Most people will notice and be grateful for your attention. Then they wish to return the favor and want to hear what you have to say—which moves them to Listening.

2. *Being memorable*—Those who believe others are listening carefully to them tend to remember more about the experience.
3. *Gathering good information*—Listening well means you'll get good data about people: their work, their opinions, where they live, etc. When they ask about you, you'll be able to say things that have meaning for *them*. (You'll present yourself differently to an engineer than you would to a CEO.)

An adult talking with students *before* a workshop at school was a novel experience for them. So was a stranger asking them about what they wanted to do, listening to them with interest, and remembering their names. It was good for me, too. I found out who was there, made a few friends, and allayed some of my own nervousness before speaking.

Listening

By listening well, we gain their attention and increase their curiosity about us. Here's what to do next.

Say Something Interesting. We have a basic sense of who they are and what interests them. Now we must say something (written or verbal) to build on this.

Back to the cafeteria. After being introduced, I looked at this room of young people and gave a special smile to the ones I'd met. (They smiled back.)

"Ask any of the adults here how they feel about writing their *own* résumés," I started. "If they're honest, they'll give you a look like a cat hawking up a furball. *Nobody* likes to do this! In fact, some of us are probably here tonight to help with *your* résumé so we can avoid looking at our *own!*

"But to get a job—especially for you, who are launching your careers—we *have* to do this. How can we make it less awful?

"Let's shift gears for a moment. I want all of you to shout out the name of your favorite superhero!" The first brave person was a boy who'd talked with me. "Black Panther!" he called out. This was followed by Wonder Woman, Spider Man, Iron Man, Supergirl, and others. I looked at them and repeated what they said, which showed my attention to and interest in them.

"Great answers all," I said when they were done. "An even *better* answer would be *you. You* are your favorite superhero. Because you have at least one talent or skill that *none* of your friends and family have!"

This was *not* the direction they expected we'd go. Now they were giving me lots of eye contact.

Play Back What You Heard. One of the most powerful things you can do now is to paraphrase: repeat the same words someone just said to you. It seems simple, but we usually mess this up for two reasons.

First, we mistakenly believe it's foolish. People often tell me, "Someone just said, 'I'm angry with you!' and I'm supposed to say, 'You're angry with me.'? That's just being repetitious!"

What we don't get is most people don't listen well, so *can't* repeat what they *should* have heard. Your ability to do this gives others the great feeling that you care about them and what they say.

Second, we tend to *interpret* information rather than repeat it. Instead, use that person's exact words—rather than substituting your own (and the judgments that go with them). It's the equivalent of answering someone who just said, "I'm angry with you!" with "You're *always* angry with me!" We've all been ticked off by someone who twisted our words. That's counterproductive in a situation that may already have its own emotional landmines.

Paraphrasing also gives us clarity on what someone intends. There's an apt quote from U.S. President Richard Nixon, "I know you believe you understand what you think I said, but I am not sure you realize that what you heard is not what I meant." Paraphrasing ensures everyone is clear about and agrees on what's happening, while giving the person speaking a chance to correct any misunderstandings.

While my talk at the Chicago Math and Science Academy wasn't a typical conversation, I still used paraphrasing.

"This is what I heard two students mention earlier tonight about *their* superpowers," I explained. "You know who you are—but I won't call you out by name, in case that's embarrassing.

"One is great at online research—knowing where to look for information and check sources to make sure they are credible. Another can do complicated formulas in their head that would take most of us a calculator and at least a few minutes. Guess what? Some company would be darn lucky to have them use these gifts at *their* place of business."

Even the teens I *hadn't* talked with knew I paid attention to their peers. Recognizing those students gained me credibility for honoring (and not embarrassing) people. This also reinforced my point—by giving an example—that everyone in the room had a superpower.

Show Your Interest. We move people from Listening to Considering by showing we care in these ways:

1. *Stay focused on them*—It takes energy not to let your mind wander, so you can paraphrase not only what you're *hearing*, but what you're *experiencing* (through listening for understanding and empathy).
2. *Listen without interrupting*—You may think you know the answer or where they're going. Then you may have the urge to finish what they're saying before they say it. *Remember: this is* you *trying to look smart rather than focusing on* them. Keep listening—no one likes to be cut off (even if you're correct).
3. *Ask questions about what the person is saying*—Your objective is to ensure you understand their ideas, issues, emotions, and

situations. Paraphrasing gets you part of the way. Asking good questions allows you to draw out new ideas.

4. *Use body language that mirrors the other person's*—Let your mirror neurons work for you. Have a stance that is a bit more open and relaxed than the other person's.
5. *Avoid giving advice*—This is the biggest misstep people make in the Listening stage: thinking they know enough to solve a problem. The truth is no one likes to be told what to do and, until you know more, you haven't earned the right to make suggestions.

I hadn't yet asked the students to do anything, because we'd been in the relationship-building phase. Now they were ready for my request.

Considering

This is the point where we move people from "yes, but ..." to simply "yes." These techniques help you get there.

Convey Rather than Convince. The original goal for students was to create their résumés. Rather than *convince* or *cajole* them to do this (you know how well *that* works with teenagers!) I conveyed a different way to look at the process.

"You already heard about two other people's superpowers," I said. "Let's take some time to think about what *you* do better than anyone else you know."

Some people scribbled in their notebooks or typed in their devices. Others looked at the ceiling or stared into the distance. Some cradled their chins in one hand and furrowed their brows in thought.

I brought them back. "That boring résumé that you weren't so excited about starting tonight? How about reframing it as a one-page graphic novel, where you get to tell people stories about *your* superpower!"

Conveying is great when you're dealing with someone you don't know or a person you need to move to action. Here's where most of us screw up. We think it's our job to *convince* people to do what we want. Not so! In part, because doing that can make us feel and look a little desperate, and few things are more unattractive. And—let's face it—once we have to convince someone to do something, we've already lost the opportunity.

Instead, convey the reasons why what you suggest will 1) help people solve a problem or 2) get what they want. This is much more worthwhile for all sides. You are speaking from your place as an expert, with ideas that are tailored to their needs. Then you're not a used car salesperson, pressuring others into something they don't need. Their resistance goes down, and they're more likely to consider what you recommend.

Show Why Their Objections Really Aren't So. Research indicates 60% of people say "no" to a new idea an average of four times before they say "yes." Their objections usually focus on these areas:

1. We have no money
2. We don't need this
3. We don't need it *now*
4. We don't trust you

They're usually not blunt enough to say the last one and may give you another reason as a smokescreen. Knowing this, you may take two courses of action to be more effective in the Considering stage.

One: Don't just think of the top *four* objections they could raise on your recommendation—consider the top *eight*. Then be ready to show why these really aren't the deal breakers they might think.

Sales coach and motivational speaker Brian Tracy offers one of my favorite twists on this. He calls it the "Instant Reverse" to closing a sale. When your potential customer says, "I can't afford it," you respond with "That's exactly why you need it!" Then you follow this with some logical reasons why that is true, such as the cost will never be lower than it is now. If the prospect says, "I'm not interested," you counter with "That's exactly why you should do this! Our best customers weren't interested when we first approached them, and now they're very happy. Their skepticism helped them get the most from what we offer." This requires some chutzpah, but it's guaranteed to turn the conversation in a new direction.

Two: Preempt objections by answering these in your conversation, memo/proposal, or presentation. Do it in a matter-of-fact way. This reduces the chances that people might get concerned about a problem they hadn't yet thought about until now.

For me, the process started before that evening's program began: knowing their preconceived notions of "a boring old lady," and the idea writing résumés isn't fun. My keynote factored in both those issues.

Make It All About Them. We usually run into two obstacles here, because our egos get involved.

We want to show that we know. Before coming to a new business meeting, for example, we've spent time learning things about our products and services and wish to share this. Unfortunately, sometimes we're so focused on sharing our knowledge and showing how smart we are, that we don't even notice everyone's eyes are glazing over.

This is a reminder that we can get so lost in *what we want to say* that we totally miss *what people need to hear*. They'll generally give us clues—or tell us outright. But if we're stuck in pushing information at them, we'll miss our chance.

We seek comfort, not success. Persuasion in general—and sales in particular—can be anxious territory. To minimize our discomfort, we go for what's familiar. In a new business situation, that could be talking about good old product features or detailed descriptions of what we do. This may soothe *us*, but it doesn't do much for those we're trying to reach.

This approach also can have the unfortunate effect of talking people *out* of the next step, of Willing to Do. They're ready to move ahead with our idea—and yet we're still talking. And talking some more! They can lose patience with us—as they should, for not paying attention to them—and throw out the idea, along with us.

THE BIGGEST MISPERCEPTION ABOUT PERSUASION

Most people believe persuasion is binary. Others say yes or no to us, and that's it. The Persuasion Cycle shows this is a process. To get someone's buy-in requires us to move them through Resisting to Listening, to Considering. When we do it well, this either creates "no" (because the fit isn't right for some reason) or Willing to Do.

What happens when people often say "no" four times before saying "yes"? That's usually a breakdown between Listening and Considering. Asking the simple question, "Is there anything I could have said or done that would have allowed us to move forward with this?" is a good move. Chances are they'll tell us, "You didn't explain ..." or "I can't see how this solves our problem/gets us to where we need to be ..."

It helps if we reframe this as they're telling us what's missing, and now we have the chance to address that issue.

My good luck with the students came from understanding three things. One: they were going to resist me because they 1) didn't want to be there, 2) thought I'd be boring, and 3) believed résumé writing would be a chore. Two: I needed to get a good sense of who they were in advance, by talking to them—showing I cared, and this program was about them—to move them into Listening. Three: to make the résumé process more interesting, in a language they understood, to move them into Considering then Willing to Do.

As I finished speaking, the cafeteria was fizzing with energy. Students focused on what made them special. They spoke animatedly with each other about their superpowers and how they would share that in their one-page graphic novel.

If this process can motivate teenagers, imagine how successful it will be with the people in *your* life!

WHAT YOU KNOW

- Before you can persuade anyone, you need to know the steps their brains go through to agree with you: 1) Resisting, 2) Listening, 3) Considering, 4) Willing to Do, 5) Doing, 6) Glad to Do, and likely 7) Willing to Do Some More.

- Persuasion isn't a "yes" or "no" thing. It's a process. The Persuasion Cycle shows you only need to move people along to the next step—rather than immediately convert them to your point of view.

- The buy-in part of the cycle is Resisting/Listening/Considering. If you can't get people through this, you don't have a chance to persuade them. They'll develop buyer's remorse and make you go through that portion of the process all over again.

- To move people from Resisting to Listening, use the *Seven Second Rule* to remember their names, then listen first (using listening for understanding and empathy).

- To move people from Listening to Considering, say something interesting or unusual, play back what you heard, and show your concern.

- To move people from Considering to Willing to Do, convey rather than convince. Address their objections and show why these aren't deal-breakers, and make it all about them.

- To uncover the reason behind one of the four "no"s you're likely to get before a "yes," ask your version of "Is there anything I could have said or done that would have allowed us to move forward with this?"

WHAT TO DO NOW

Practice Persuasion Awareness Exercise

1. List three events this week that require you to persuade someone to do something. These could be meetings, phone conversations, or something you write. (***Explore*** in the Open Mindset Signal™.)

   a. ______________________________

   ____

   b. ______________________________

   ____

   c. ______________________________

   ____

2. List where that person is/those people are on The Persuasion Cycle. (***Explore***)

   a. ______________________________

   b. ______________________________

   c. ______________________________

3. Identify the tactics for moving them along to the next stage. (***Go*** in the Open Mindset Signal™.)

   a. ______________________________

   ____

   b. ______________________________

   ____

   c. ______________________________

   ____

4. Afterward, write what you tried and the results you got. (***Go***)

   a. ______________________________

   ____

   b. ______________________________

   ____

   c. ______________________________

   ____

5. How was this different from just "winging it"? (***Explore***)

   a. ______________________________

b.

c.

6. What *didn't* work as well as you'd hoped, and what did you learn from this? (***Explore***)

   a.

   b.

   c.

7. What turned out *better* than you expected and is worth doing the next time you face a similar situation? (***Go***)

   a.

b. ______________________________

____

c. ______________________________

____

S = SHOWCASE

CHAPTER 8

Know What to Say

Too often we hone our messages to a fine gloss, deliver them to expected applause, and instead hear crickets. Here's the main reason for that.

Ben was the new president and CEO of a company of skilled care nursing facilities in Indiana. His business coach suggested Ben strengthen his employee communication skills: "Spend a day with Lynne."

Ben did the MIND Reader Method™ personality inventory in advance. His two primary styles were Igniter and Mover, closely followed by Detailer, with Nicer a distant fourth. That meant he was well suited to working with his private equity board. Ben could 1) present his ideas in an engaging way, 2) provide enough information to help them make informed decisions, and 3) easily answer questions when they wished to drill into the details behind the company's performance. Ben also was an inspiring leader to his direct reports.

His difficulty lay in connecting with many of the people working in the organization. Healthcare attracts a good percentage of Nicers. They focus on caring for people and valuing emotions, are afraid of being left out, and aren't as concerned with deadlines and accuracy.

All of these were wonderful qualities for the residents and families they served. However, skilled care nursing is a highly regulated business. There are forms and reports required for compliance, good ratings, and Medicare/Medicaid coverage. Ben was frustrated that these areas of the operation weren't running smoothly enough. There was the related matter of revenues being lost when ratings didn't reflect the company's quality of care, and compliance records weren't done on time.

As Ben shared these issues, we worked through new approaches he could use. At the end of the day, he agreed to try these, shook my hand and thanked me for my insights.

A few weeks later, Ben called. "Can I get a regular dose of you to keep me on track with all this stuff?" he asked.

When we met in December, I asked him, "What's the gift you'd like to give this company as its leader—not just now as president, but even after you're gone?"

"I want to create a culture of collaboration," Ben said. "We have 23 different facilities. I love how the executive directors at each building run these as though it's their own business! The problem is that Building 1 could have a great program for onboarding new employees, and Building 2 could be struggling with that. They'll never talk to each other, and everyone hates Corporate. How much more could we achieve if we worked together?"

At my request, Ben gave me a copy of his financial and operational goals for the coming year. I promised to create an internal communication plan where every message and activity tracked back to meeting one or more of those goals, plus "We have a culture of collaboration." Then I went to work.

MESSAGES ALWAYS START WITH GOALS

We created three overarching goals, with measurable objectives for each:

1. Improve quality
    - Each facility receives a 4 or 5 star quality rating by year's end (15 currently did; 8 ranged between 1–3)

2. Meet or exceed the financial budget
    - (This included specific targets, such as 1) percent increase in total revenue, 2) percent increase in expenses, 3) profit versus prior-year loss, 4) total number of patients in care, and 5) labor cost control goal)

3. Create a culture of collaboration:
    - Ensure employees understand and support current vision and values statements:
        1. Mission: To share our passion for improving quality of life through innovative healthcare—one person, one family, and one community at a time.
        2. Values:
            a. Make integrity and accountability your pledge
            b. Share our passion for excellence
            c. Be uncompromising in delivering quality care

    - Work with employees to identify and agree on the qualities of a culture of collaboration
    - Recognize and reward employees who live the mission and values, and promote the agreed-upon culture of collaboration

CREATING MESSAGES THAT WORK

Those goals gave us focus and direction. Next, we needed to decide what to say to help everyone work together to get there. We followed my Meaningful Message Process™ by answering six key questions.

Step #1: Who are the different audiences involved?

Here was the "everyone" we identified: 1) board of directors, 2) senior leadership team, 3) executive directors (who run each facility) and directors of nursing services (also at each facility), and 4) all direct care and support employees. (External communications were being done by an outside agency. I needed to keep them informed and coordinate messages that were shared with patients and their families, the local community, and the media.)

Step #2: What does each audience think of you (if they know you) and your company? Do they like and trust you? Do they see you as different from your competitors?

The idea is to know two things. First, are there any plusses we can capitalize on—such as do they know Ben and trust him? Second, are there any obstacles we must overcome—such as they have no connection with Ben yet, or they had a poor experience with him or with the company? After interviewing a sample of each group, here's what I discovered:

1. *Board of directors:* They were impressed with Ben's background and industry experience. Because he'd been there less than a year, they were still looking for signs that he was the right person for the job. In addition, the chairman was very abrupt and confrontational, so other directors were watching to see how Ben would handle him.

2. *Senior leadership team:* Some predated Ben at the company. They were feeling out his leadership style and deciding if they wanted to stay. Others had been hired by Ben and also were finding their way in a new team. The general sense was positive, with some "wait and see."
3. *Executive directors and directors of nursing services:* Most had been in these positions before Ben arrived. They were nervous because of rumors the company might be sold or broken up (because it was operating at a loss). They had been unhappy with the amount of interference by—and lack of resources from—prior senior leadership and the board. They had seen some positive progress since Ben's arrival but were skeptical if this would turn into long-term positive change.
4. *Direct care and support employees*: They were always asked to do more with less and expected Ben would continue this approach. They were keeping their heads down and doing the work to serve patients and hold onto their jobs—while having an eye on other places they might go if the company's fortunes changed.

Step #3: Put yourself in each audience's place. What do they want to know about working with you and your company?

We can get so caught up in what *we* want to say that we don't even consider what *others* need to hear. It's useful to spend time seeing things from their perspective. And it's always a plus when more than one audience wants to know the same thing.

My research revealed these areas of interest for each group:

1. *Board of directors:*
    a. What will you do to help the business grow and return to profitability?

b. Are you the right leader, including holding your own with an outspoken chairman who is a micromanager?
c. How good are you at motivating a decentralized operation?

2. *Senior leadership team:*
    a. What kind of leader are you?
    b. Will you be open to my ideas?
    c. Are there opportunities for me to advance my career here?
3. *Executive directors and directors of nursing services:*
    a. Will you offer support and resources to help me tackle my biggest challenges, including attracting and keeping good people to serve our patients?
    b. Will you continue to give me the independence I need to make good decisions at my facility for my staff and patients?
    c. How will you help with the overwhelming amount of documentation we must complete to stay compliant with industry regulations?
4. *Direct care and support employees*:
    a. When will you give me the resources I need to do my job and serve patients well?
    b. What can I do to move up in the company?

Step #4: Bring the focus back to you. What do you really want each group to know about you and the company?

While you want to make sure each audience's communications needs are met, that doesn't mean you ignore your own messages. You have goals for this company and there are ideas you need to share to reach these. This is what Ben wanted each group to know.

1. *Board of directors:*
    a. I am the right leader for the company
    b. I have a solid vision for its future

c. I have the industry experience and skills to motivate others to work together to reach our annual and strategic planning goals

2. *Senior leadership team:*
   a. I'm a fair and collaborative leader
   b. We have a good plan for the company's growth and the support of the board to get there
   c. You are a valuable member of the team and have opportunities for further growth here
3. *Executive directors and directors of nursing services:*
   a. I worked my way up in this industry and am familiar with the challenges you face at your facility, so I know what you need to serve patients and meet corporate goals
   b. The board and I are committed to giving you the resources to meet the goals we set and appreciate your abilities to run your facility like it's your business
   c. We will put new systems and processes in place to help you achieve the necessary quality and compliance standards
4. *Direct care and support employees*:
   a. The board and I value your hard work with patients and their families and want to support you in doing this
   b. There is a path to advance in your career here
   c. We are committed to paying competitive wages for your work

Step #5: Review the last two steps. What are the common ideas: the messages each audience needs to hear, and those you want to share?

As you have seen, there were a number of areas where the needs of Ben's audiences and the points he wanted to make to them overlapped:

1. He is the right leader to handle the needs of the board while providing the resources for each facility to reach financial and operational goals
2. The company has a sound plan and will be around for the long term
3. The culture we're fostering supports listening to ideas to improve operations, recognizing good people, and offering them opportunities to grow
4. New systems will be implemented to reduce the burden of compliance and reporting

It's rare that there is no intersection between what people want to hear and what you wish to tell them. When this *does* happen, it's time to investigate your motives for communicating. Is this a difficult conversation where you'd rather not tell someone what he wants to hear? Are her wishes so different from yours that your goal is to change her mind? Communication is tough when there is little to no common ground. Many times it's up to you to find it—or to create it first.

Step #6: What are the three most important messages? What are the proof points or supporting strategies needed for each?

You already know the Rule of Three Ideas: this is the maximum number the brain can easily process (Chapter 3). The blessing of creating three main messages is that it helps us focus on what's most important.

In addition, having three supporting points for each of your messages shows you thought through your position and have come prepared. Since your goal is to persuade people, you can use these sub-points to preempt some of their objections in advance.

Ben and I looked at the "common ground" messages in Step #5. Then I helped him prioritize these into the top three for each audience. We separated these into two groups: 1) the board and 2) everyone who worked in the company. This would make it easier for us to share consistent messages with all employees. Here was the result, with supporting points:

Board of directors messages:
I can successfully lead the company

1. **Ensuring we offer quality service:**
   a. Providing relevant education and training
   b. Setting clear expectations for performance
   c. Monitoring and reporting on key performance indicators and holding people accountable
2. **Ensuring we provide excellent care:**
   a. Improving patient satisfaction
   b. Improving performance so more facilities achieve CMS 5 Star ratings
   c. Improving areas mentioned in the regulatory survey
3. **Creating sustainable financial outcomes:**
   a. Increasing rate utilization with Medicare and Medicaid
   b. Controlling expenses
   c. Improving labor efficiencies

Internal Audiences Messages:
We are creating a culture of collaboration, based on a trusting work environment with a leadership team that's "in it for the right reasons"

1. **The company is stable and has a bright future**
   a. We created significant improvements to date this year, giving us a strong foundation to make more progress
   b. The board has committed to reinvesting in our operations (including regulatory and quality compliance systems)
   c. We will actively manage changes in the business environment on regulatory guidelines and federal reimbursement programs

2. **You are appreciated and valued**
   a. We recognize and reward outstanding performance
   b. We seek your feedback on important company-wide decisions
   c. We give you the authority and support to run the business as if it's your own
3. **You have opportunities to grow**
   a. We want to know and help you achieve your professional goals
   b. You earn additional opportunities by performing well in your current position
   c. We urge you to take advantage of training and education programs to help you reach your goals faster

Too many times we think of messages as an "either/or" prospect: either we say what *others* want, or we talk about what *we* want. From now on, use this process to create a "both/and" situation: the people you're trying to reach get their needs met *and* you don't have to ignore what you want to say to make that happen.

TANGIBLE PROOF THAT MESSAGES WORK

Knowing what we wanted to create, and what to say to each group to get there, made it easy to develop Ben's internal communication plan. We only needed to decide how and when to deliver our messages.

This began with enhancing how he was already reaching out, including board meetings, and Monday virtual sessions with executive directors and directors of nursing. We reviewed messages and determined what should be shared, and how to answer questions to encourage dialogue on key topics.

We provided new experiences to bring people together. One example was a company-wide training, which included an interactive session on corporate culture. This created two important results. The first was a word cloud—an image where the words employees most often used to describe the culture appear in larger type. A graphic of this was posted in the lobby of each building to remind employees of their shared values. The second was a discussion guide for executive directors to use when talking about the culture at their facility.

Ben was thrilled with the results at the end of the first year:

1. The company was profitable and far exceeded its financial goals
2. The company met all operating goals
3. The employee survey showed a statistically significant increase in satisfaction, and employee turnover was dramatically reduced
4. Directors were pleased with Ben's stewardship, and employees felt more seen/heard/recognized by corporate and facility leaders

Knowing what to say, how to say it, and doing this consistently does more than make you persuasive. It makes a difference in your world—and the people who share it.

WHAT YOU KNOW

- When developing messages, always start with your goals:
  1. What's the change we want to create?
  2. What measurements can we use to know whether or not we've seen those changes?
  3. Having these in place gives us a good foundation for determining what to say.
- Use a six-step process to create messages that not only work for the people you're trying to reach, but you, too:
  1. ***Identify your audiences.***
  2. ***Ask what each audience thinks of you*** (if they know you) and your company. Do they like and trust you? Do they see you as different from your competitors?
  3. ***Put yourself in each audience's place.*** Make a list of what they want to know about working with you or your company.
  4. ***Bring the focus back to you.*** Make a list of what you want each person to know about what you provide or the company offers.
  5. ***Review the last two steps and list the common ideas***—the messages each audience needs to hear, and you want to share. (If there isn't any common ground, discuss why this is so and what to do about it.)
  6. ***Narrow your messages to three*** (to make this easier for you and your audiences to remember). Develop up to three proof points or supporting strategies as needed for each.

WHAT TO DO NOW

Six Steps for Developing Messages Exercise

Pick a communication event—a presentation, proposal or report—and use these steps to get clear on what you want to say: (***Explore*** In the Open Mindset Signal™.)

1. Identify your audiences.

   a. ____

   ____

   b. ____

   ____

   c. ____

   ____

   d. ____

   ____

2. What does each audience think of me? Of the company? Do they like and trust me? Do they see us as different from our competitors? (***Explore***)

   a. ____

   ____

   b. ____

   ____

c. ___

___

d. ___

___

3. What do they really want to know about this subject? (***Explore***)

   a. ___

   ___

   b. ___

   ___

   c. ___

   ___

   d. ___

   ___

4. What do I really want to tell them? (***Explore***)

   a. ___

   ___

   b. ___

   ___

   c. ___

   ___

d. ____

5. What are the common ideas between #3 and #4? (***Explore***)

6. What are the top three messages from #5? What proof points or strategies can I share to support them? (***Go*** in the Open Mindset Signal™.)

   1.

      a.

      b.

      c.

      d.

2.

a.

b.

c.

3.

a.

b.

c.

S = SHOWCASE

CHAPTER 9

Tell Strategic Stories

*Our brains are designed for stories.
Good ones are like a Trojan horse.
They slip past resistance in our thinking
brain and speak directly to our emotional
brain, which is where we make decisions.*

"We are the best-kept secret in Chicago," said David, the founding partner for a regional law firm. "I want you to create a program on storytelling for our next partners' retreat, because I want our lawyers out there telling our story."

I smiled. "Your lawyers *don't want* to tell your firm's story," I explained. "And if you tell them they're coming to a program on storytelling, they'll drag their heels the whole way. But if you say we're going to explore and use the world's best practice development approach, they'll show up for *that*. Fortunately, it's storytelling!"

You saw what happened. I changed David's message of "this is what you *have* to do" to "this program gives you a skill to build your practice"—something every partner *wants*.

David agreed. This chapter is your crash course on that full-day experience.

WHY STORIES WORK

There are few groups more skeptical than a room filled with lawyers. That made showing the neuroscience behind storytelling the place to start. By sharing facts that support this approach, we'd move away from "this is Lynne's opinion" (rife for dispute) to "here's what scientific research says" (making it easier for them to agree).

Our Brains Are Wired for Stories. That's because 100,000 years ago, we used stories to pass along information. About 27,000 years ago, those stories were augmented with cave paintings. Written language is only about 3,000 years old, with illuminated manuscripts appearing some 1,400 years ago, and printed books are roughly 500 years old.

Dry Facts and Bullet Points Invite Listeners to Resist Us. Presenting our ideas in this way activates only two parts of the brain. First is the angular gyrus, which helps us recognize language. Second is Wernecke's area, which helps us to understand words and concepts. Both are located in the thinking brain. This means we are inviting the people to resist us. That would be the reaction we get when saying, "*I* was standing on a beach." (Their response? "Who cares!")

Good Stories Speak to Our Emotional Brains. This is important, because it's where we make decisions. We believe we make decisions in our thinking brain—and we're full of crap. We make decisions emotionally, then use the thinking part of our brain to rationally explain that choice.

Here's how we know. The physical structure that corresponds with the emotional brain is the limbic system. Research shows when this is injured, people can't decide something as simple as "do I want the red pen or the blue pen?"

We start to speak to people's emotional brain when we make the story about *them*. That would be the reaction we get from saying, "Imagine *you* are standing on a beach."

Great Stories Sync Listeners' Brains with Ours. Research shows our brains can't tell the difference between something we *imagine* or *remember,* and something that's actually *happening*. The neurons in our brains fire ("light up" on functional MRI scans) in the same way, as if we're experiencing something right now!

What's fascinating is the brains of people listening to you light up as if *they* are going through the same experience! Their brains are firing in sync with yours, which means you're connecting on a molecular level.

The more parts of a brain that are engaged, the lower the resistance is to what we're sharing. Studies also show that people accept ideas more readily when their brains are in story mode versus an analytical mindset (those facts and bullet points).

That would be the reaction we get from saying, "You see the sun glinting on the incoming waves." (Visual cortex is activated). "The smell of coconut suntan lotion from nearby sunbathers wafts through the air" (olfactory cortex). "You wiggle your toes in the sand, then sink a little lower each time a wave covers your feet" (motor cortex). "Children are laughing and splashing in the water" (auditory cortex). "You feel the warmth of the sun on the back of your neck and a little sweat on your upper lip" (somatosensory cortex).

You were *there*, weren't you? And open to hearing more.

CHOOSING THE RIGHT STORY TO CONNECT

Here's the biggest mistake we make when telling stories. We want people to like us, laugh with us, commiserate with us, and like or dislike the same people or situations we do. That's all about *our* ego, not connecting with *them*. We can shift this by telling stories strategically to meet those goals we set (back in Chapters 1–3).

I think the biggest benefit of a story is that we let listeners/readers *come to their own conclusions* about what's happening. This gets them involved in what's going on and beats *telling* them what to think, feel, or do—every time. It also creates less resistance, moving them along the Persuasion Cycle.

My favorite approach to this comes from consultant, speaker and author Annette Simmons.[13] She identified six stories we can share to bond with others. Let's dig into what we want each story to accomplish, how to use it, and see an example of it in action.

Type	Goal	Use
"Who I Am"	Break down preconceived notions or judgments about you and your motivations	Reveal a flaw or mistake to make yourself more human and approachable

Example: *How do you immediately increase the comfort level of a group by showing that you also have fears, mess up, and learn from both?*

When people ask how I got into persuasive communication, I tell this story.

---

13 Simmons, Annette. *Whoever Tells the Best Story Wins: How to Use Your Own Stories to Communicate with Power and Impact.* ANACOM 2007 updated 2024.

Fred was a 14-year-old standing three feet in front of me. I couldn't tell you anything about him, except he was holding the world's largest machete. He yelled, "You try to call for help, I'll cut you!"

I was the only adult in a boy's group home. Fred ran away two days ago. He broke the rules by showing up here, so I thought it was my job to tell him what do to. "Fred: you can't be here. You have to go to Intake, tell them what you've been up to, and have them clear you first."

Fred grumbled, "No: I'm going to my room."

I said, "We can do this the easy way or the hard way, just go to Intake."

He raised his voice. "No. I'm going to my room!"

I went to the staff office to call for backup, so someone could be with the other boys while I worked with Fred to get him to Intake. Fred followed me into the room, zipped open his backpack, pulled out the machete and cut the phone cord—my only lifeline with the outside world. He growled, "You try to call for help, I'll cut you too!"

All I could do was babble. "Fred: I like you … you like me … and you don't want to hurt me." Fred's scowl showed he wasn't agreeing with any of this. So I kept babbling. "And you don't want to get into the world of hurt you're going to get into if you hurt me!"

Fred blinked. Later, he told me he started thinking about how his life would look if he stabbed me. The police would drag him off and lock him up. All I saw was the blink and somehow knew this was my chance. I stuck my hand out and said, "Fred, just make it easy on yourself and give me the knife." I was scared he'd bring the knife down and chop my hand. But I knew I needed to keep it out there. To show Fred I thought he was a good kid and give him the chance to act like it. I can't tell you how long I stood there, sweating through everything I had on, until Fred finally sighed and gave me the knife.

He also gave me two abiding gifts that day. First, an interest in how to reach unreachable people. Second, the litmus test for my job. As long as no one pulls a machete on me I'm having a good day!

Type	Goal	Use
"Why I'm Here"	Replace suspicion with trust and prove you don't have a hidden agenda	Show you're a good person and want to work with others to achieve a common goal

Example: *How do you grab an audience's attention by making your company's story about them?*

Shaunna was the treasurer of a public company that provided in-flight internet services. Her boss, the CFO, asked her to speak at a debt conference in his place. She had never been in a high-profile situation—presenting to a room of investors—and wanted my help to prepare.

"When are you speaking?" I asked.

"At 9:00 on Wednesday morning," she said.

"How long will the conference have been going on by then?"

"This is the third and final day," Shaunna said.

"These people will be pie-eyed—after two days of CEOs and CFOs shoving boring information at them. We have to do something right away so you stand out, and they won't tune out." Here is what happened.

Shaunna stood before them and asked, "How many of you flew to get here, or have flown recently?" She raised her right hand, showing them how to respond. Already this was different: few presenters had asked the audience to interact with them. Many hands went up.

"How many of you were reading emails or streaming videos on the flight?" She raised her left hand, and a good number of them did the same.

"I'm betting you thought, 'Gee, the internet on this plane is slow. It was a whole lot faster when I did this three years ago. And I'm about to go to a conference where [company name]—the people who are responsible for my pain—are going to speak. I'd love to give them a piece of my mind!"

The audience smiled and laughed. Shaunna knew she had them.

"You're absolutely right," she continued. "Bandwidth in the air hasn't changed in three years, while the number of users has exploded exponentially. That's the bad news. The good news is we used this time to create a new platform that provides speeds in the air as fast as those in your office. We're rolling that out this year. That means we can build on our 50% market share in the U.S.—because no one else has a system that can compete. And the same thing is true internationally, so we plan to see explosive growth in our 3% share there."

At the end of her talk, Shaunna was swamped with investors who wanted to speak with her. She was thrilled. "This is far more than I *ever* saw approach the CFO after *he* spoke!"

Type	Goal	Use
Teaching	Demonstrate an idea in a memorable way	Make a lesson clear and help people remember why they are doing something

Example: *How do you, as a subject matter expert, make a less knowledgeable group feel comfortable trying something frightening?*

Connie's IT firm helped clients choose a software platform to make their operations more efficient, then move their data into it. She was giving a session at a conference for her new target market: not-for-profits.

"What do you know about your audience?" I asked.

"Two things that can be deal breakers," she replied. "First, most of them can't afford an IT person, let alone a department. Second, as a result, they're confused and frightened by the process of migrating their data onto a new system."

"Neuroscience has good news for you," I told her. "When you connect something that seems *complex* with something that seems *simple*, you reduce resistance to that new idea."

We put this to work, calling her session "Can You Make a Hot Dog? Then You Can Use IT to Save Money and Attract Donors."

She started her talk with, "I get it. No one wants to move to a new IT platform. It seems overwhelming—especially if you don't have a technical background or in-house staff for support. But the people your organization serves need your help, and you need to reach donors to fund your good work. You know that a new system will make all your efforts more efficient. How can we make this easier?

"Here's the truth. If you know how to make a hot dog, you know how to implement a new software system. I'll prove it! What's the first thing you do when you're making hot dogs?"

Someone shouted, "Go to the grocery store and buy the ingredients!"

"Right!" Connie said. "You have to gather the hot dogs, buns, and condiments (no ketchup—this is Chicago!). The same thing is true with an IT system. You need to pull together all the data that will go into it. Like client lists and donor lists. The good news is you already have all this stuff—so you don't have to go to the store."

She took them through each step of the process, using the hot dog analogy: firing up the grill, making sure it's ready, putting on the hot dogs, watching them cook, then enjoying the taste with those around you.

By the end of her session, Connie's audience felt more comfortable with being able to move into a new software platform. A good percentage talked with her about how she could help them do this.

Type	Goal	Use
Vision	Inspire hope	Stimulate action and raise morale by reminding people of their ultimate goal in working together

Example: *How do you share bad news in a caring way?*

The new president of a major office products distributor reviewed the company's operations. He discovered a prior leadership team's commitment to expansion had left the company with too many old, inefficient warehouses. He presented a plan to the board on how to improve the facilities, which was approved. Unfortunately, one building near Detroit had issues that couldn't be solved and would need to be closed.

How could this news be shared with the associates there—and throughout the organization—recognizing the pain and changes it would cause?

Our first focus was the people in Detroit: union and non-union employees. To develop and deliver messages as respectfully as possible, we made these choices:

1. Dennis the facility director—someone known and trusted by the associates—would deliver the news in person. To help him feel as prepared as possible, Dennis and I had a number of speaker training practice sessions so he felt ready.
2. His message, delivered during shift change on a Friday, was straightforward:
    a. We did a company-wide facility study and determined that, despite all your hard work and productivity, this center couldn't be brought up to efficiency standards.

  b. There were three reasons: 1) it is one of the oldest, and we discovered it would cost more to upgrade it than to build a new more flexible facility; 2) it is landlocked and can't be expanded; and 3) there are other more effective facilities in Michigan that have additional capacity.
  c. Those facts, combined with a slowdown in the industry, are forcing us to close.
  d. This is frightening news for all of us. Yes: I'll be out of a job, too. How are we going to get through this together? It may help to know we are taking several steps to support associates with this transition:
     1) We'll provide all the separation benefits that reflect our company policy to non-union associates. For our union people, we'll begin effects bargaining next Tuesday to determine the separation benefits you'll receive.
     2) [He offered details on they would be informed on benefits and whom to contact with questions.]
     3) Yes: positions are available at [another facility] if you'd consider moving and want to apply there.
3. Then Dennis acknowledged the consequences of this decision—practically and personally:
  a. [He explained how this would start affecting day-to-day operations beginning on Monday]
  b. We realize how much this announcement affects everyone. So we're giving you the rest of the day off, to go home for the weekend. You'll be paid for today. When you return to work on Monday, we'll share more details on the part you'll play in closing the facility.
4. Dennis gave a personal commitment to earn trust during the process:
  a. You have my promise to keep you informed about what's happening.

   b. If you have questions, please see me or your supervisor at any time on any topic.
5. He ended with sincerity:
   a. It's an honor to be here with you. I hope we can work together—as we always have—and help each other get through this on the way to the next step in our careers. Thanks for everything, and I'll see you on Monday.

Dennis' open and frank comments—and continuing commitment to answering associates' questions—showed people his goodwill. There were no demonstrations or picket lines, no disgruntled employees calling the media or others in the company, and the facility was closed on schedule.

Type	Goal	Use
Values in Action	Explain what a value really means	Clarify an intangible (such as "integrity") in a working relationship or situation

Example: *How do you show how your values drive your behavior?*

Early in my career, I was an account executive (AE) with the world's largest public relations agency. It was common for people in leadership or at other offices to charge small amounts of time across many clients. This was designed to boost their billable hours for the month. The AE on the account generally would pass this through unchallenged. It was seen as not worth the hassle, especially if you wanted to build alliances and move up.

But I'd promised my clients to be a good steward of their budget. Each month, I reviewed the time and expense sheets to ensure the bills they'd receive were correct—and that we were spending their money to meet their program goals.

When a charge appeared for something I didn't request or know about, I'd call to ask for details. "I have to write the monthly program report that goes with the bill," I'd explain. "Can you tell me what you did so I can include it?" If there was a good explanation, that's what I'd do. Most of the time, they'd say it was a mistake and be OK with me removing the charge. The bonus for me was that after a month or two of this, they'd stop.

This wasn't the case with a media relations exec in New York. Let's call him Meyer. In answer to my first call, Meyer treated me like an idiot.

"You obviously don't know how media relations works," he sniffed. "I go out to lunch with reporters and pitch a number of client story ideas. They write about the ones that will interest their readers, and that's how companies get coverage. So I charge for the time I spend pitching your clients."

"Great," I said, trying not to sound huffy. "Can you tell me which reporters you pitched last month so I can put them in my report?"

"Look. I pitch a lot of story ideas and have a lot of meetings with reporters. I can't tell you off the top of my head which ones I presented your client to," he replied.

"Would it help if I gave you time to check your records?" I asked.

"I'm too busy for that! Everyone who's savvy in this agency never questions my hours," Meyer retorted.

"Fine," I said. "Can you tell me what angle you pitched for my client and what kind of response you got?"

"This is crazy!" he sputtered.

"I understand your frustration. Tell you what. Why don't you come up with a plan of whom you're going to contact, the story you want to pitch them on, and how you'll follow up. Then you can let me know about the progress you're making, and everyone will be well served."

Meyer hung up on me.

He charged more hours the following month. I called again and left a voicemail, which he didn't answer. I cut his hours from the bill. He didn't dispute the change and never charged hours to my clients again.

Later, a colleague mentioned going to Meyer's office for a meeting. Once Meyer realized this man knew me, he showed him the back side of his office door. This featured a dart board, over which Meyer had tacked a picture of me that had plenty of darts sticking out of my face.

None of my clients heard this. It was enough for me, and those I prevented from billing fake hours, to know that's what stewardship meant.

Type	Goal	Use
I Know What You're Thinking	Show respect for others' viewpoints while sharing your own	Recognize objections and then show why they don't apply

Example: *How can you show that someone's worst-case scenario won't happen?*

Bill had been hiding in his office for weeks.

He was the manager of an automotive parts manufacturing plant. Everyone there knew corporate headquarters was trying to sell the operation. Bill was afraid to talk with employees.

"What can I say when they ask why they're selling us?" Bill asked our team of consultants. "What can I do if they get angry and blame me for not running the place well enough so the company would *want* to keep us? How can I look in their eyes when they say, 'I've worked here my entire career. My father worked here before me. How will I ever find another job?'" His eyes were wide with terror and pain.

We'd just completed a communication audit of his facility. This involved doing interviews, focus groups, and surveys to determine how information moved—and didn't—at Bill's plant. We were going to present our findings to his employees, then have Bill talk about the plan we worked with him to create on how to improve communication.

"You think everyone blames you, Bill," I told him. "But we've been listening to your people. They think you're a straight-shooter and respect you. But they've noticed you're not walking around the building anymore, so they're guessing it's worst-case scenario time. This is your chance to show you care about them. Yes: you can expect tough questions. We'll work with you in advance on ways to answer these. But when you tell your people the truth, you'll find a lot more supporters than haters. I believe this is going to turn out better than you think."

The morning of the meeting with employees, Bill's face was shiny with sweat. When it was his turn to speak, he clenched the podium. He had a hard time looking up as he made his points.

When Bill was done, he quietly called for questions, hoping for none.

A punch press operator stood up. "We know the plant is for sale," he said. "I just want to thank the company for taking the time and spending the money to do this report anyway. And to tell us what you're going to do to make things better here." As he sat down, many employees clapped to show they agreed.

Bill's eyebrows rose in surprise.

A theme emerged in the Q&A that followed: "What can we do to make our plant more attractive to a potential buyer?"

I watched Bill. It was like seeing an iceberg melt. He went from a corporate stiff behind a podium, to a man walking among people he wanted to work with. Bill felt the goodwill in the room. He was touched by the dedication of people who wanted to do a good job to make the business more viable.

As the meeting ended, Bill said, "We're all in this together." He was surrounded by people who shook his hand and pledged to do their best.

Bill did what he promised, and employees rose to the challenge beside him. The plant's quality and productivity improved, while expenses were cut. The business attracted a purchaser that was impressed with these results and wanted to keep the people who created them.

BACK TO THE ROOM OF LAWYERS

Remember the retreat where lawyers were learning to use storytelling to expand their practices? Each practice group got together over lunch and created their own strategic story. (The two most popular were "Why I'm Here" and "I Know What You're Thinking.") Then they chose a representative to tell the story to the rest of the partners.

The lawyers learned from watching each other tell their stories—the techniques that worked and those that fell flat.

Evaluations showed the partners rated this as the firm's best retreat. More importantly, the session led to two sustainable changes.

First, lawyers throughout the firm began using stories to explain what they did and the results this created. Potential clients began to see how this attorney was different from those at other firms—in a way they could understand. This led to more new business. In addition, current clients heard that their attorney (supported by others in the practice) handled a wider range of issues than they thought. Clients started sending more business to their attorney, as well as referring their attorney to others.

Second, the attorneys discovered what professionals in the other practices were doing. For example, real estate attorneys began to understand what was happening in reinsurance. That boosted the number of referrals passed between practices.

This ultimately gave David, the founding partner, what he wanted: attorneys were out there telling the firm's story. But they did it in a way that no longer bored or alienated the people they were trying to reach.

THREE NEXT STEPS

Here's what to do now:

1. Start building a portfolio of stories. Begin with brainstorming ideas (with freewriting or mind mapping), then develop the best ones, so you have these ready when you need them.
2. Use stories to *show*, not tell. This lets people reach their own conclusions rather than experiencing it as a lecture.
3. It may be *your* story, but make it about the people who are seeing/hearing/reading it. Do that by involving them: pick the right type of story, include details that engage different parts of their brains, and feel free to reference your audience.

WHAT YOU KNOW

- Our brains love stories:
    1. Humans have used stories to share knowledge for 100,000 years, which has shaped the way our brains are wired.
    2. When we present dry facts and figures, these appeal to the thinking part of the brain—leading people to resist us.
    3. Good stories bypass that resistance by speaking directly to our emotional brains, which is where we make decisions.
    4. Great stories actually sync our listeners' brains with ours, increasing their receptivity to our ideas.

- Annette Simmons identified six types of stories we can tell strategically to connect with and persuade others:
    1. ***Who I Am stories*** share a personal flaw to break down preconceived notions about us and show we're human and approachable.
    2. ***Why I'm Here stories*** build trust by showing we don't have a hidden agenda and are here to work with others to achieve their goals.
    3. ***Teaching stories*** share an idea in a memorable way to help people understand why they're doing something.
    4. ***Vision stories*** inspire hope and raise morale by showing why we're working together.
    5. ***Values in Action stories*** take an intangible idea and show what it means from the perspective of the person telling it, so others can agree or share their definition.
    6. ***I Know What You're Thinking stories*** show respect for others' views and illustrate why their objections to our ideas don't apply—then can help create new ideas or approaches.

WHAT TO DO NOW

Understanding the Power of Story

Reread the "Who I Am" story in this chapter. (***Stop*** in the Open Mindset Signal™.)

1. What was the mistake I made? (***Explore*** in the Open Mindset Signal™.)

   ____

   ____

2. What did you learn about me? What qualities describe me? (***Explore***)

   ____

   ____

   ____

3. Did you think any less of me because I shared a failure? Why? (***Explore***)

   ____

   ____

4. If we'd just met, and I told you I had the qualities you wrote, would you believe me? (***Explore***)

   ☐ Yes ☐ No

Why?

____

____

____

You've now experienced the power of *showing* versus *telling*. When you allow people to reach their own conclusions about you, they're more likely to believe these—than if you just stated "I am ..."

Creating a Strategic Story

1. Pick a situation you'll face in the next week (Zoom/in-person/phone) in which you'll want to connect with one or more people. (***Stop***)

   ____

   ____

2. What's the result you want this conversation to create? (***Explore***)

   ____

   ____

3. Which strategic story will best help you do this: (***Explore***)

   ☐ Who I Am ☐ Why I'm Here

   ☐ Teaching ☐ Values in Action

   ☐ Vision ☐ I Know What You're Thinking

4. Brainstorm ideas for stories that have happened to you and fit into this category: (***Explore***)

   a. ____

   ____

   b. ____

   ____

   c. ____

   ____

   Circle the one you believe is the best choice.

5. Start developing this story: (***Explore***)

   a. What's the main takeaway you want others to get from this?

   ____

   b. Who was involved?

   ____

   ____

   c. What was the situation/issue?

   ____

   ____

d. What happened?

e. What was the result?

6. Why is this important for them/her/him to know? (***Explore***)

7. Speak it out loud: record it and play it back to yourself. Answer these questions to make it better: (*Go* in the Open Mindset Signal™.)

    a. How many minutes was it? What can I take out to make it more succinct (include cutting out verbal clutter like "um" and "uh")?

    ____

    ____

    ____

    ____

    b. What can I do to make this more about the listener(s)?

    ____

    ____

    ____

    ____

    c. How can I give this a more attention-getting start?

    ____

    ____

    ____

    ____

d. How can I make the ending more compelling?

8. Practice this with people whose opinion you respect and ask them to answer the same questions. Put their best recommendations here. (***Go***)

AFTERWORD

Put It All Together

Using PersuasionGPS™—in part or in whole—allows you to be the best version of yourself as you help others also get more of what they want.

Reading most or all of this book is like spending several days of training with me. Here's what I say to groups when they reach this point.

"You've discovered a lot of new ideas, and you're excited about using them! Maybe you've already made a promise to yourself on what you're going to do differently.

"Now you're about to encounter the most powerful force in the universe. *Inertia!* You'll go back to work (or home) and immerse yourself in the tons of things you need to do. In a few days, you'll likely think, 'What was it I was going to try? I'm too busy now and will get back to it next week.'

"The truth is that if we don't take action within a week of learning something new, chances are good we *never* will. Inertia can feel so comfortable—because it doesn't require us to change—that we default to it, no matter how dissatisfied we are with the status quo. How can we break through this?"

Break out the Open Mindset Signal™:

- ***Stop*** relying on cruise control and "close enough." Decide where your biggest barriers or greatest opportunities are. Then pick one.
- ***Explore*** the chapters on that topic. Consider new ideas, or enhancements of ones you've used. Circle back to the sections on Goals to make sure you're setting meaningful ones for yourself.
- ***Go*** try new approaches! Be gentle with yourself. You're human and won't get everything right the first time. Ask for help from those you trust.

As you get more comfortable with your persuasive communications, it's easy to think you know it well. Or you don't have time to look up something. That's a fast-track to falling back into old thoughts and actions—inertia. Here's another set of tools to help.

The next nine pages are simple, practical checklists for you! They are a digest of everything we've covered, in order, so you can 1) take PersuasionGPS™ from beginning to end for a particular situation, or 2) focus on a useful group of techniques to enhance what you're already doing. This is how to use it.

1. Do a quick scan of the checklists now.
2. Note which areas you already do well. Circle the title on ones with new ideas or actions you can improve. Play with those (using the list here or exercises after the chapter).

3. When you really want to be persuasive, use all these sheets to prepare your entire approach.

You are at your most powerful and persuasive when you know why you're here, what you want, and how to connect with others to make that happen. This book shares my best ideas for doing that.

You placed a lot of trust in me and invested a lot of time in yourself. I'm honored to be on this journey with you. Know that I want *more* for you. Let me know the results you're getting from using PersuasionGPS™. And know I'm here to support you if you have questions—or need a nudge in the right direction for you!

CONNECT WITH ME

I'm available for speaking, workshops, coaching, consulting, and interviews.

- www.LynneFranklin.com
- Lynne@LynneFranklin.com
- 1-847-729-5716
- www.LinkedIn.com/in/LynneFranklin

GOALS CHAPTER #1 CHECKLIST:

Find Your Mind or Help Others Do the Same

Are you stressed out or in a crisis? Or are you dealing with someone else in this state? Identify where you/they are, and follow the process for getting your/their brains back.

1. What stage am I/are they in *now*, using Goulston's "Oh F#@& to OK" process:
   a. ***Reaction Phase:*** "There's no way I can fix this. I'm so screwed!"
   b. ***Release Phase:*** "I'm going to get stuck fixing this. Why does this stuff always happen to me?"
   c. ***Recenter Phase:*** "This is lousy, but I'm not alone. I know people and have resources to help me deal with this."
   d. ***Refocus Phase:*** "I'm not going to let this ruin my life!"
   e. ***Reengaging Phase:*** "I'm ready to start dealing with this."

2. What's the next action I need to take to keep myself or others moving through this?
   a. ***Reaction Phase:*** Start moving past flight, flight, freeze, or fawn by answering, "What am I feeling?"
   b. ***Release Phase:*** Breathe deeply and admit that it sucks and that you're going to have to do this yourself.
   c. ***Recenter Phase:*** Remind yourself that you're not alone, you're resourceful, and start getting your thinking brain back.
   d. ***Refocus Phase:*** Use your anger in service to yourself, helping you to get your emotional and thinking brains working together.
   e. ***Reengaging Phase:*** Your thinking brain is back in full force, and you're ready to start strategizing on what you can do immediately to deal with the situation.

GOALS CHAPTER #2 CHECKLIST:

Use Goals to Rewire Your Negative Brain

Just because you have gotten your brain back, there still are negative thoughts that can shoot you in the foot. Bring these into focus, so they don't attract the wrong outcome from your subconscious mind.

1. What's my biggest negative thought that tells me I can't get what I want in this situation?
2. What triggered this thought?
3. What facts support the truth of this thought?
4. What facts disprove it?
5. How would my life change if I no longer believed this?
6. What positive thought do I want to replace this with?

GOALS CHAPTER #3 CHECKLIST:

Create Goals that Motivate Your Brain

The more clarity you can give your conscious and subconscious minds about what you want, the more likely you are to get it.

1. Write your *communication goal*: the general result I want to create (for myself and others). Use these ideas to get started:
   a. *Inform*—to share information
   b. *Request*—ask for something
   c. *Record*—tell people about a meeting or event that has already happened
   d. *Instruct*—tell people how to do something
   e. *Persuade*—get people to do something
   Then:
   f. What's my point?
   g. Why does it matter?

2. Brainstorm your *action goals*: what you will do to make your communication goal come true.
   a. Use freewriting or mind mapping: whichever works best for you
   b. Pick the top three ideas this generates.
   c. Write your communication goal and place your three action goals beneath it (use this as a handy reference to focus your attention).
3. List the likely breakdowns that could prevent you from reaching your goals. Strategize on what you'll do if these surface.

PEOPLE CHAPTER #4 CHECKLIST:

Be Aware of Your Unconscious Biases

We jump to conclusions about people all the time—because our brains are trying to quickly fill the gaps in our knowledge and keep us safe. Be aware of which unconscious biases may affect your behavior.

1. Honestly assess which of the 11 "people biases" may affect your thoughts and actions (see Chapter 4 for definitions):

___ Affinity	___ Ageism	___ Attribution
___ Authority	___ Beauty	___ Gender
___ Halo effect	___ Horns effect	___ Idiosyncratic rater
___ Names	___ Racial	

2. Do the same with "decision-making biases":

___ Affect heuristic	___ Anchor	___ Confirmation
___ Conformity	___ Contrast effect	___ Illusory correlation
___ Overconfidence	___ Regency	___ Status quo

3. How will you watch for these in this situation?

4. What will you do when you notice you're acting this way?

PEOPLE CHAPTER #5 CHECKLIST:

Understand Personality Styles

When people act differently than we would, we often jump to a judgmental conclusion. Knowing the four basic personality styles can help us stay focused on who people are *rather than making them* wrong.

1. According to the MIND Reader Method™, I believe this is my primary style:
   ____ Mover
   ____ Igniter
   ____ Nicer
   ____ Detailer

2. I believe the person/people in this situation is/are:
   ____ Mover
   ____ Igniter
   ____ Nicer
   ____ Detailer

3. This means we agree upon [what].

4. This means we may clash:
   a. They want [what] and I want [what]
   b. They value [what] and I value [what]
   c. They're afraid of [what] and I'm afraid of [what]

5. How can I present my ideas in a way that connects with this person/these people?

PEOPLE CHAPTER #6 CHECKLIST:

Pay Attention to How People Think

People process information in three ways. You can build rapport faster when you know two things. First, how they like to receive ideas. Second, when you mirror their body language.

1. This is my dominant approach to processing information processing information:
   ____ Looker
   ____ Listener
   ____ Toucher

2. I believe the person/people in this situation are:
   ____ Lookers
   ____ Listeners
   ____ Touchers

3. This means we may clash:
   a. On eye contact: They want [what] and I want [what]
   b. On physical space/contact: They want [what] and I want [what]
   c. On appearance: They want [what] and I want [what]

4. What types of words (visual/auditory/feelings and tactile) can I use to build rapport?

5. What kind of body language should I be aware of and mirror to increase their/his/her comfort?

SHOWCASE CHAPTER #7 CHECKLIST:
Know Where People Are in Being Persuaded

You'll treat people differently depending upon where they fall in Goulston's Persuasion Cycle.

1. I believe the person/people in this situation is/are in this phase:
   ____ Resisting
   ____ Listening
   ____ Considering
   ____ Willing to Do
   ____ Doing
   ____ Glad to Do

2. What should I do to move him/her/them to the next step (you're concentrating on moving from Resisting to Listening to Considering to Willing to Do):
   a. Stay focused on them
   b. Listen for understanding and empathy (without interrupting)
   c. Ask good open-ended questions that relate to what they're saying
   d. Paraphrase what they say (using their words)
   e. Notice if they're Lookers, Listeners or Touchers and use appropriate verbal/written/body language
   f. Avoid giving advice
   g. Anticipate their objections and show why each isn't a problem
   h. Make it all about them (rather than showing off my knowledge)
   i. Ask for a conversation
   j. Ask for a meeting
   k. Ask for the opportunity to do a proposal (whatever your process for getting an approval is)

SHOWCASE CHAPTER #8 CHECKLIST:

Share Engaging Messages

Most messages fail because they're about us rather than the people we want to reach. Use this simple system to create meaningful messages that still allow you to convey what others need to know.

1. What are the names of the people I want to reach?
2. What does each person think of me? (What can I leverage and what must I overcome?)
3. What do *they* want to know about my idea/topic?
4. What do *I* want to tell them?
5. Where do #3 and #4 overlap?
6. What are the three most important points from those in #5, in order of significance?

SHOWCASE CHAPTER #9 CHECKLIST:

Tell Stories that Connect

Every story should support your goals and messages, while focusing on something of interest to the person you want to reach. Draw upon the six stories created by Annette Simmons.

1. Which kind of story best supports reaching the goal(s) I have for this interaction?
   a. ***Who I Am*** – break down preconceived notions or judgments about me
   b. ***Why I'm Here*** – replace suspicion with trust to show I don't have a hidden agenda
   c. ***Teaching*** – demonstrate an idea in a memorable way
   d. ***Vision*** – inspire hope
   e. ***Values in Action*** – show what an intangible value means
   f. ***I Know What You're Thinking*** – show respect for others' viewpoints while sharing my own

2. Which of my stories best fits this situation? (Use freewriting or mind mapping to brainstorm then select a good story.)

3. Tell this story to those I trust and get their feedback on what can be improved.

ABOUT THE AUTHOR

After a boy threatened to kill her with a machete, Lynne Franklin started learning all she could about persuasion.

As a "neuroscience nerd," she translates how the brain works into practical strategies that fast-track leaders to be seen, heard, and promoted. This includes her proprietary approaches to better connect with others:

1. PersuasionGPS™ system—a favorite of those who want to achieve big goals or break through barriers
2. MIND Reader Method™ personality profile to quickly identify what people value, fear, and how to best reach them
3. TEDx Talk on "How to Be a Mind Reader" that went viral with millions of views (www.tinyurl.com/LynneTEDx)

Lynne creates a fun space for executives, rising stars, teams, and association members to improve their productivity, profits, and career prospects. Past president of the National Speakers Association Illinois Chapter, Lynne wrote the book *Getting Others To Do What You Want.*

Can your organization no longer afford miscommunication between leadership and employees, between departments, or within a team? Would 1:1 communication coaching help you reach your next level of success? Seeking a lively keynote speaker for an event? Contact Lynne at 847-729-5716, Lynne@LynneFranklin.com, https://tinyurl.com/Talk2Lynne, www.lynnefranklin.com, or www.linkedin.com/in/lynnefranklin.

> ***"I don't care what your company or audience for your association is. Lynne will give every person in the room ways to communicate better, ways to become more engaged, ways to connect. And keep your group so entertained it's just amazing. Hire Lynne Franklin. You will not be making a mistake!"***
>
> *—Rick Davis, President, Building Leaders Inc.*

DID YOU ENJOY THE BOOK?

If you got something useful from reading this, please help me by 1) suggesting it to someone you think might benefit from it, and 2) leaving a positive review on Amazon. Your comment will assist others who are looking for ways to be more persuasive. Thanks in advance for taking a few moments to do this for me.

You may also be interested in my first book, *Getting Others To Do What You Want*. If you haven't read it yet, get your copy today at Amazon.

Thank You!

ACKNOWLEDGEMENTS

There's an irony about writing a book. While my name appears as author, so many people stepped up to create what you see.

Thanks to all my beta readers and proofers: Laurie Carver, Dan Creinin, Kathy Dvorak, Denise Hansard, Dawn Metcalf, Melody Mulaik, Jeff Rogers, Ellen Schnur, Cindy Skalicky, and Craig Smiddy. You challenged fuzzy thinking, found, typos, and always made it your goal to improve what you saw. I also value the graphic work done by Larry Pecorella in picturing my ideas.

Then there are the true believers, who said, "I want to read this book!" and encouraged me when my focus or energy flagged. I'm grateful to you Ron Anderson, Christine Boos, Mary-Beth Esser, Mark Franklin, Mary Griffin, Holly Kahan, Delinda Layne, Cathy Pisano, Karen and Kris Thalhammer, and Susan Thurston-Hamerski.

My appreciation goes out to all of those researchers on neuroscience, persuasion, and communication who taught me new ideas and challenged some of my old ones. Here are just a few (who are in my bookcase): Robert Cialdini, Lisa Feldman Barrett, Daniel Kahneman, Mark Goulston, Leonard Mlodinow, and Annie Murphy Paul.

Finally, thanks to all the clients who trusted me to be their consultant, coach, speaker, and workshop facilitator. Your openness to new ideas and behavior inspired me, and your stories touched and encouraged me.

www.ingramcontent.com/pod-product-compliance
Lightning Source LLC
Chambersburg PA
CBHW071327120626
46546CB00002B/478

* 9 7 8 1 9 5 3 1 8 3 7 8 1 *